Know with Certainty

by Randy Harshbarger

© 2021 One Stone Press – All rights reserved.

All rights reserved. No part of this book may be reproduced in any form without written permission of the publisher.

Published by:
One Stone Press
979 Lovers Lane
Bowling Green, KY 42103

Printed in the United States of America

ISBN 13: 978-1-941422-61-8

www.onestone.com

Contents

Foreword	7
Introduction	9
Nature of Faith	11
The Birth of Jesus	13
The Virgin Birth	15
Jesus in the Temple	17
Jesus Begins His Ministry	19
Jesus Begins His Ministry: The Spirit of the Lord	21
Jesus Begins His Public Ministry: A Prophet Without Honor	23
Levi, the Tax Collector	25
Lord of the Sabbath	27
The Beatitudes	29
John the Baptist	31
The Woman Sinner	33
Women in the Kingdom	35
The Transfiguration	37
What Must I Do to Inherit Eternal Life?	39
A House Divided	41
The Sign of Jonah	43
Woe on the Pharisees	45
Bigger Barns	47
Christ the Divider	49
Repentance	51
Invited Guests	53

Scripture quotations taken from the (NASB®) New American Standard Bible®, Copyright © 1960, 1971, 1977, 1995, 2020 by The Lockman Foundation. Used by permission. All rights reserved. www.lockman.org

The Prodigal Son. 55
Faithful in Little or Much. 57
Ten Lepers. 59
Pharisees and Publicans 61
Zacchaeus 63
By What Authority? 65
Things to Come. 67
The Lord's Supper 69
Simon of Cyrene 71
He Has Risen 73
You Shall Be My Witnesses 75
The Resurrection of Christ 77
The Holy Spirit 79
Repent and Be Baptized 81
Added to the Church 83
Silver and Gold 85
Opposition to the Gospel 87
Barnabas 89
Ananias and Sapphira 91
We Must Obey God 93
Serving Tables. 95
The Preaching of Stephen 97
Stephen's Preaching #2 99
Stephen's Preaching #3 101
Stephen's Preaching #4 103
They Stoned Stephen. 105
Philip the Evangelist. 107
Simon the Sorcerer 109
The Ethiopian Eunuch 111
The Ethiopian Eunuch #2. 113
Saul of Tarsus 115
Saul Meets Jesus 117

Saul and Ananias.	119
Cornelius.	121
Peter's Sermon to Cornelius	123
Peter's Sermon to Cornelius #2.	125
Christians in Antioch	127
A Praying Church.	129
The Voice of a God Not of a Man.	131
The Church at Antioch.	133
Words of Wisdom.	135
Barnabas, Paul, Zeus, Hermes	137
Acts 15 and Bible Authority.	139
Acts 15 and Bible Authority #2.	141
Acts 15 and Bible Authority #3.	143
Acts 15 and Bible Authority #4.	145
Acts 15 and Bible Authority #5.	147
The Church at Philippi	149
Thessalonica: A World Turned Upside Down.	151
Corinth: The Church of God	153
Ephesus: The City of Diana	155
Acts 20: Upon the First Day of the Week.	157
Acts 21: I Am Ready to Die	159
Acts 22: I Am a Jew, Born in Tarsus.	161
Acts 23: Hope and Resurrection of the Dead.	163
The Convenient Season.	165
Paul Before Festus.	167
The Hope of Israel.	169
I Believe God	171
Now When We Come to Rome	173

Foreword
by Dee Bowman

I am pleased to recommend Randy Harshbarger's *Know with Certainty*. It is filled with excellent information showing the coming of the kingdom and the function of the early church in fulfillment of the command to make disciples of all nations.

The gospel of Luke is a book of antecedent action. It contains vital information regarding the coming of Jesus Christ and what He did to introduce the kingdom which was promised for the salvation of mankind from the beginning of time. It tells about Him—about His birth, His relationships with the people of His time, about His Jewish detractors and His confrontations with them, about His choices for His apostles, about his horrible treatment, his death and his resurrection.

The pivotal passage which joins Luke and Acts, is Luke 24:46-47. "And said unto them, Thus it is written, and thus it behooved Christ to suffer, and to rise from the dead the third day: And that repentance and remission of sins should be preached in his name among all nations, beginning at Jerusalem."

In *Know with Certainty*, Randy has produced what I have chosen to call an exposition/application commentary. He is faithful to the text in his exposition of every context, but he doesn't leave out the application. On every page there is vital exposition , but he does not stop there. Every exposition is followed by some timely application. He gives you something to take home with you.

Randy Harshbarger is a gospel preacher. He has filled his life with the distribution of the gospel message. He has done outstanding local work—the last few years at the Stallings Drive Church of Christ in Nacogdoches,

Texas. He is highly reputed for his foreign work in such difficult areas as Ethiopia. This new work is a tribute to his faithfulness and dedication to the gospel of Jesus Christ.

Introduction

Each week for the last twenty-seven years I have written a "new" bulletin article for use in our local teaching program here at Stallings Drive, Nacogdoches. Even though writing on Bible themes is serious business, I have never imagined that my brief offerings would find much interest beyond the confines of our work here. Only occasionally did someone use some of these articles in other forums. I have enjoyed trying to write in ways that might cause some reflection and further study; that desire might be too ambitious. Still, I hope you get some good out of these articles.

I thank Marc Hinds for his design work on the book's cover. Marc is extraordinarily gifted in publishing ventures; beyond that, he is a good student; and more, he is my friend. My thanks also go to Warren and Paula Berkley for their encouragement and guidance in this project. Their expertise in editing, formatting, etc., makes this book possible. I thank the Lord for their friendship and encouragement. Thanks to Andy Alexander (a former Texas boy!) for taking a flyer on this book. He is a good businessman and knows what he is doing.

Thanks to my longtime friend and encourager, Dee Bowman. Dee has prodded and motivated me to write and then has commended my efforts in ways that helped and kept me going. I have learned from Dee that "writer's block" will just not do. Life is too short to waste time in getting ready to write; write! Thanks Brother Bowman.

As always, thanks to my wife Marilyn, who remains a constant source of love and help and hope. Her perennial question is, "Did you get anything accomplished in the office today?" When I answer, "Not much, but I did write a bulletin article," she says, "Good." There are lots of good things in my life.

—**Randy Harshbarger**

CHAPTER 1

Nature of Faith

"Inasmuch as many have taken in hand to set in order a narrative of those things which have been fulfilled among us, just as those who from the beginning were eyewitnesses and ministers of the word delivered them to us, it seemed good to me also, having had perfect understanding of all things from the very first, to write to you an orderly account, most excellent Theophilus, that you may know the certainty of those things in which you were instructed."
(Luke 1:1-4)

Christians are people of faith. Faith saves, faith justifies, faith directs the walk of all who seek to follow Jesus (Ephesians 2:8-9; Romans 5:1; 2 Corinthians 5:7). "The faith," the objective body of truth known as the New Testament, drives the subjective, personal faith of God's people (Jude 3; Ephesians 4:5). It is also true that faith, whether "the faith" or one's personal faith, binds believers to the same conclusions about Jesus Christ. That is what Luke is writing about. Luke, "the beloved physician," was not the only person looking into and seeking explanation about Jesus of Nazareth. Writing to Theophilus (a title, a real person?) Luke, as a trained medical man, was able to provide an eyewitness account of this divine narrative; he performed an autopsy; he saw with his own eyes. What Luke examined would be added to what Theophilus already knew; "certainty" was Luke's goal. Can we, too, examine Luke's account and have certainty about who Jesus is? Where does Luke's gospel come from? In the 1st century there were eyewitnesses and ministers of the word; the apostles and others had direct contact with Jesus. Paul said that some actually saw Jesus after His resurrection (1 Corinthians 15:6). These people could provide firsthand information about Jesus and His life. This information was delivered to "us," Luke and others, a second generation of believers.

Luke "investigated everything carefully from the beginning" and then wrote his findings "in consecutive order." Now Theophilus could "know the exact truth about the things you have been taught" (Luke 1:3-4 NASV). Think of an explorer seeking the source, the headwaters of a mighty river. Where does the river begin? How can one follow its course? Theophilus could do that after being taught and after learning more about Jesus Christ. Luke was accurate in his work. Would we expect less than that from a trained doctor? We want our doctors to be careful and precise before they operate, don't we? A careful study of Luke's gospel (or any other gospel) will reveal a plan, or pattern, or scheme, by which the reader can see the orderliness of the message.

Luke is concerned with certainty. He wanted Theophilus to be firm and stable in his faith. He wanted Theophilus to know that the truth about Jesus was undoubted truth. This would prevent and protect Theophilus from spiritual dangers. To know Jesus is to get Him deeply in our hearts. Yes, we know what the Bible says. But we need to know of whom the Bible speaks. Will this come from subjective feelings? From some emotional experience? From our loved ones? No! We know about Jesus by getting in His book and examining what He says. In this case, by examining what Luke is writing about.

CHAPTER 2

The Birth of Jesus

> "And it came to pass in those days that a decree went out from Caesar Augustus that all the world should be registered. This census first took place while Quirinius was governing Syria. So, all went to be registered, everyone to his own city. Joseph also went up from Galilee, out of the city of Nazareth, into Judea, to the city of David, which is called Bethlehem, because he was of the house and lineage of David, to be registered with Mary, his betrothed wife, who was with child. So it was, that while they were there, the days were completed for her to be delivered. And she brought forth her firstborn Son, and wrapped Him in swaddling cloths, and laid Him in a manger, because there was no room for them in the inn."
> (Luke 2:1-7)

The question, "When was Jesus born?" is asked by many, especially so, because of the religious world's celebration of Jesus' birth on December 25. While the Bible nowhere commands that we celebrate the birth of Jesus, we might ask if there is evidence of some kind that relates somehow to the time of His birth? Luke's passage includes three references to historical figures. Even if you do not believe the Bible, these people are in the history books; weigh the evidence and decide if you believe that these persons really lived. Augustus Caesar, the nephew of Julius Caesar, ruled the Roman Empire from 27 BC to AD 14. Quirinius was governor of Syria from 10 BC to 6 AD. Matthew 2:1 refers to Herod the Great, half Jew, half Idumean, who was appointed ruler by Rome in 40 BC; he reigned until AD 4. What shall we conclude? It is clear that Jesus was born into a particular historical framework; Luke's attention to detail places Jesus's birth in the context of the Roman Empire. And it is clear that Jesus was born before Herod the Great died. Still, the Bible does not say that Jesus was born on December 25. Luke 2:8 says, "Now there were in the same country shepherds living out in the fields, keeping watch over their flock by night." An angel told the shepherds that Jesus, the Savior, Christ the Lord, had arrived. Some argue that since the shepherds were watching over their sheep by night, this would not have been in December, a typically harsh and cold month. Whether yes or no, we are still looking for something that might point us to December 25. The shepherds went to Bethlehem, found the newborn baby, and then told others about what had happened; others were interested in the report of the shepherds. They did not say, though, that they had gone to Bethlehem on December 25.

If we do not celebrate the birth of Jesus on December 25 each year, do we celebrate His birth at all? We should rejoice and be thankful that Jesus did come to this earth. Just because the majority of the "religious world" is on shaky ground in celebrating Jesus' birth on December 25, that doesn't mean that we cannot and should not be just as happy and thankful as anyone else might be in the fact that Jesus, born of a virgin, did come and die for all (Hebrews 2:9-10). His death frees us from the bondage of death (Hebrews 2:14-15). His birth fulfills prophecy; wouldn't this be of interest to Luke who was writing an accurate account of the life of Christ? Rather than when did Jesus come, let us ask: Why did He come? When we figure that answer out, we can then go beyond December 25 in our commitment to our Savior.

CHAPTER 3

The Virgin Birth

> "Now in the sixth month the angel Gabriel was sent by God to a city of Galilee named Nazareth, to a virgin betrothed to a man whose name was Joseph, of the house of David. The virgin's name was Mary."
> (Luke 1:26-27)

Luke's narrative has moved from the temple in Jerusalem to Galilee. Zacharias' vision that his wife, Elizabeth, would bear a son, brought fear and incredulity. When Zacharias asked, "Could it be true?" his lack of faith rendered him without speech until the baby came. Then the same angel, Gabriel, appeared to Mary, bringing her news about another baby. How could this be true, "since I am a virgin?" Gabriel answered, "The Holy Spirit will come upon you, and the power of the Highest will overshadow you; therefore, also, that Holy One who is to be born will be called the Son of God" (Luke 1:35). Mary's virginity, while integral to the story, would not be a problem. A son will come; but not just any son. Mary's son will be called "the Son of God." He would be *the* son, to whom all the world is summoned to bend low in worship and praise and thankfulness. Luke believed in miracles. He said Jesus would be born of a virgin; the angel said so; and now Luke records that truth; there was no hedging on his part, no, well maybe this or that. We believe in miracles, too, don't we? That is, we believe what the Bible says about the birth of Jesus. A virgin was betrothed or engaged to Joseph; her name was Mary; she said she was a virgin. But now, she is going to have a child. Layer Luke's account with Old Testament prophecy about the virgin birth of Christ. Isaiah 7:14 says, "Therefore the Lord Himself will give you a sign: Behold, the virgin shall conceive and bear a Son, and shall call His name Immanuel." The prophet said the same thing Gabriel said: a virgin would conceive and have a son. The birth of Jesus was normal; the conception of Jesus was supernatural.

This son, born of a virgin, would save people from sin (Matthew 1:21). Can we be saved, really saved, from sin? Is salvation a reality or a myth? While unbelievers deny the virgin birth and its consequences, the Deity of Jesus is exclaimed loudly by the events surrounding the conception and birth of the Savior. He is the "Son of God." He is King on David's throne, ruling in His eternal kingdom. Yet, He was born of a virgin; He lived as a man among men. How did He make His advent into this world? Through the virgin birth.

Impossible you say! Not with God! Faith in the virgin birth shows our respect for God's word. The Bible says this is what happened. We either believe what Luke said, or we don't believe. Do we want to be saved from sin? If we believe we can and will be saved through Jesus, then how can we turn in disbelief from His virgin birth? Why accept anything Jesus said? Why obey anything He commanded? "Then Mary said, 'Behold the maidservant of the Lord! Let it be to me according to your word.' And the angel departed from her" (Luke 1:38). *According to your word.* Mary believed what the angel said. Do we?

CHAPTER 4

Jesus in the Temple

"His parents went to Jerusalem every year at the Feast of the Passover. And when He was twelve years old, they went up to Jerusalem according to the custom of the feast. When they had finished the days, as they returned, the Boy Jesus lingered behind in Jerusalem. And Joseph and His mother did not know it."
(Luke 2:41-43)

The stupendous nature of Jesus' life and works defy even the best of our abilities as we struggle to imagine and comprehend at least something about Jesus of Nazareth. Evidently, others felt the same way (John 21:25).

Still, the trip Jesus and his family took to Jerusalem opens a few doors of understanding about our Savior. Joseph and Mary had little concern about where Jesus was as they began their trip home. In the 1st century loved ones, relatives, and neighbors acted as surrogate parents to young children. Joseph and Mary assumed that Jesus was safe and sound, located somewhere in the group that had traveled to Jerusalem together and now traveled home together. Imagine the concern of Joseph and Mary as they returned (alone?) to the city and then searched (frantically?) for three days until finally they found their son. Their concern turned to joy.

Joseph and Mary found Jesus in the temple. We have already been with Luke in the temple; remember Simeon and Anna? The one who is greater than the temple now sits in the temple, listening and asking questions of the Jewish teachers—those skilled in the Law. The temple was often criticized by Jesus. In fact, if the Jews could not get beyond their attachment to the physical temple, that structure would be destroyed. The experts were astonished as they listened to Jesus. Mary asked: Why have you done this to us? We've been looking for you all over the place! Jesus replied, "Did you now know that I must be about My Father's business?" The first recorded words of Jesus are words about Himself. His words take us deep into the relationship between Jesus and His Father, deeper than any earthly relationship. Jesus wants all to have a relationship with Him and His Father. Is that possible? Yes, if we will be about our Father's business. What is that business? It is salvation! That is why Jesus came; that is why His Father was willing for Him to leave heaven and come to earth; that is why the Father gave His Son to die for the world. Salvation is heaven's business; saved ones invest their lives in the kingdom?

Jesus' parents didn't quite get the point of what their son said. Still, Mary quietly filed these events away in her heart. How often, throughout her lifetime, did she remember those frantic days spent in looking for Jesus. In one sense, Joseph and Mary lost Jesus. And we can lose Him, too. They found him; we can, too. But we have to look in the right place. We will not find Jesus among loved ones, or among the wise religious people of the world, or among the temples of our lives. We find Jesus when we go back, all the way back, to Him, His word, His life, His death. Are you ready to take that journey?

CHAPTER 5

Jesus Begins His Ministry

"And He came to Nazareth, where He had been brought up; and as was His custom, He entered the synagogue on the Sabbath, and stood up to read. And the book of the prophet Isaiah was handed to Him. And He opened the book and found the place where it was written,
'The Spirit of the Lord is upon Me, Because He anointed Me to preach the gospel to the poor. He has sent Me to proclaim release to the captives, and recovery of sight to the blind, to set free those who are oppressed, to proclaim the favorable year of the Lord.' And He closed the book, gave it back to the attendant and sat down; and the eyes of all in the synagogue were fixed on Him. And He began to say to them, 'Today this Scripture has been fulfilled in your hearing.'"
(Luke 4:16-21)

After a trip to Jerusalem (John 2-4), Jesus began His Galilean ministry; the bulk of His work would be away from Jerusalem, the temple, and the ubiquitous Pharisees. Still, Jesus' world was one of political, religious, and ethnic turmoil. Undercurrents of seething resentment from the Romans toward the Jews, from the Jews toward the Romans and Gentiles, and from the Gentiles toward the Jews, covered Palestine with the possibility of trouble on many fronts. Competing mindsets and agendas brought discussion, debates, and sometimes violence. Jesus steps into this world and says: I am here to bring peace; unite with Me in a kingdom like no other.

The origin of the synagogue is unknown. Many suggest that the synagogue originated during the time of the Jewish exile in Babylon. Nehemiah 8:1

says, "And all the people gathered as one man at the square which was in front of the Water Gate, and they asked Ezra the scribe to bring the book of the law of Moses which the Lord had given to Israel." Whether synagogue or not, what Ezra and others did, mirrored synagogue activities. Archeology has uncovered synagogues in the ancient world. More importantly, synagogues were places of community, religious, and social life for the Jews. Synagogues were used as schoolhouses, places of prayer, as meeting houses for religious activities, and as houses of judgment when the community was involved in discipline matters. Charity work, the care of orphans, and instruction in the Law were common in synagogues.

When Jesus entered the synagogue on that eventful Saturday 2,000 years ago, He had the attention of those who were steeped in Judaism. His reputation had preceded Him. And now He returns to His boyhood home. What would He say? Would He fan the flames of rebellion and rally His fellow Jews in rebellion against Rome? The message of Jesus was revolutionary, His kingdom was of a different kind. Would He work a miracle that would "put Nazareth on the map"? What could Joseph's son do for the citizens of Nazareth? Nothing? But what could the Son of God do for those sitting in the synagogue with rapt attention, eager to hear? He did for them and does for us what we can never do for ourselves. And so, why wouldn't we want to hear everything Jesus has to say? Have you been to the synagogue lately?

CHAPTER 6

Jesus Begins His Ministry: The Spirit of the Lord

> "The Spirit of the Lord is upon Me, Because He anointed Me to preach the gospel to the poor. He has sent Me to proclaim release to the captives, and recovery of sight to the blind, to set free those who are oppressed, to proclaim the favorable year of the Lord."
> (Luke 4:18-19 NASV)

The Messiah-Servant, Jesus Christ the Lord, quotes Isaiah 61:1-2, and says, "I am the fulfillment of this prophecy." The kingdom of heaven was breaking in; Old Testament kingdom prophecies were being fulfilled. Isaiah anticipated the coming Messiah when he spoke of the role of the Spirit in connection with the Messiah. "Behold, My Servant, whom I uphold; My chosen one in whom My soul delights. I have put My Spirit upon Him; He will bring forth justice to the nations" (Isaiah 42:1; 11:2; 49:8; 50:4). Jesus was anointed with the Holy Spirit (Acts 10:38); with this power and with the approval of His Father above, He would go forth and preach to the poor and bring relief to miserable people everywhere. Bringing release to the captives echoes the Year of Jubilee (Leviticus 25:10; Jeremiah 34:8), a time of release from slavery or bondage (in many forms). Isaiah also said that the advent of the Messiah would bring "the day of vengeance of our God" (Isaiah 61:2). The Messiah would bring healing; He would also bring judgment against those who rejected the Father's promises in Christ.

Clearly, Jesus worked miracles as the Messiah. His power to cast out demons, heal the crippled, and raise the dead authenticated His claim to be God's Son. Human suffering was often alleviated by His works. The greater message was salvation. That is Luke's message from the beginning. Jesus would bring "redemption," "salvation," "mercy," and "forgiveness" (Luke 1:67ff). Forgiveness, the release from the captivity of sin, lifts the heavy burden that no one can bear alone. The Day of Atonement as celebrated by Israel (Leviticus 16) restored broken relationships. A physical remnant would return from Babylon; spiritual Israel would be delivered by the atoning death of Jesus. Jesus preached the gospel, making possible a new people, a new community. These new people would come to the kingdom in contrition; they could now see and walk and speak (metaphors for spiritual healing?).

Jesus' kingdom was not the kind of kingdom expected by Judaism. The Jews knew about kings, kingdoms, war, fighting, military defeats and victories. Rome's dominion in the first century contributed to Jewish anxieties about their very existence. Will a military deliverer, such as David, come and fight for them? Jesus parables make it clear that His kingdom would be unlike any earthly kingdom. Jesus told Pilate, "My kingdom is not of the world." The Jews wanted salvation from their enemies; Luke 1:71 says, "Salvation from our enemies, and from the hand of all that hate us." But Jesus brought a different kind of salvation. If there was ever to be peace between the Jews and the Romans, or, if there is ever to be peace among mankind, then all need to be at peace with God; this must come first. Then, we can be at peace with each other. How revolutionary! How counterintuitive! But it was that kind of peace that Jesus brought to Israel and to all. Jesus, the Prince, the Savior, brought repentance to Israel and remission of sins (Acts 5:31). Now, if that is what Jesus was talking about in His synagogue, shouldn't we sit down and listen?

CHAPTER 7

Jesus Begins His Ministry: A Prophet Without Honor

> "And all the people in the synagogue were filled with rage as they heard these things; and they got up and drove Him out of the city, and led Him to the brow of the hill on which their city had been built, in order to throw Him down the cliff. But passing through their midst, He went His way."
> (Luke 4:28-30 NASV)

Jesus' manner of speaking and His message attracted great interest of those gathered in the synagogue in Nazareth; all eyes were upon Him. Most knew Him to be Joseph's son; this could be incredulity; it could simply be an obvious recognition of someone they had seen growing up in the neighborhood. If they were expecting great words and deeds from this hometown boy, they would soon be disappointed; they were soon angry beyond words. What did Jesus say that so fanned their flames of rejection?

"And He said to them, 'No doubt you will quote this proverb to Me, "Physician, heal yourself! Whatever we heard was done at Capernaum, do here in your hometown as well."'" It seems clear that the folks at home expected great things from Him. This proverb says that if you are a doctor and you prescribe medicine for the sick, then when you get sick, you will take the same medicine. If Jesus, as He claimed, was the Messiah, the Son of God, the Savior of Israel, then He would be expected to do great things right there, right then. His work in other places was well-known; now, the people say, "Do something here." He said, "Truly I say to you, no prophet is welcome in his hometown." Jesus would be rejected by His own people; what He came to do was out of step with hometown expectations. This initial ire is repeated often in Luke's narrative; especially are the leaders of the Jews singled out for their unbelief (Luke 9:21-22; 112-53).

Still, the reaction of the people in Nazareth didn't mean that Jesus wasn't a prophet sent from God; in fact, He was coming to them in the same spirit and manner of two well-known Old Testament prophets, Elijah and Elisha. Jesus was not rejecting His own people; neither were Elijah and Elisha. But God worked through these Old Testament prophets as He helped some needy outsiders. Why would God help a widowed woman, a non-Jew? Why would God reach out to a non-Jew who had leprosy? Jesus, Elijah, and Elisha brought good news and healing to those *dreaded others*. Yes, unclean Gentiles, those with no status in Nazareth, were objects of God's concern. Surely this would be welcome news to the folks in Nazareth. But, not so! The people were outraged. Forgetting that it was the Sabbath, a day on which work was forbidden, they sought to execute Jesus. They, as did their fathers, continued to reject the prophets. The gospel of the kingdom, if we allow it to do so, will change the way in which we view the world. The gospel speaks to ultimate reality for this life and the one to come. Our prejudices, our pride, our attachments to the good life, our values, all of which are predicated on our perceived self-sufficiency, must give way to the call and openness of the gospel. The despised Sidonians and Syrians would accept Jesus. His hometown neighbors would not accept Him. Will you?

CHAPTER 8

Levi, the Tax Collector

"After that He went out and noticed a tax collector named Levi sitting in the tax booth, and He said to him, 'Follow Me.' And he left everything behind, and got up and began to follow Him. And Levi gave a big reception for Him in his house; and there was a great crowd of tax collectors and other people who were reclining at the table with them. The Pharisees and their scribes began grumbling at His disciples, saying, 'Why do you eat and drink with the tax collectors and sinners?' And Jesus answered and said to them, 'It is not those who are well who need a physician, but those who are sick. I have not come to call the righteous but sinners to repentance.'"
(Luke 5:27-32 NASV)

Tax collectors in first century Palestine worked for the Roman government. Their wages were good; if they left their post, the job was lost forever; so, there were obvious benefits from sitting in the tax booth. The fact that Levi threw a party for Jesus and for others, after the Lord called him, indicates some material substance. There was also a downside to being a tax collector. The Jews lived in mutual animosity with the Romans. When a Jew sided with Rome, he risked the ire and alienation of his fellow countrymen. But this was not so with Jesus. Levi, an agent of Rome, would normally be excluded from "polite society." This would include all the tax collectors and the dreaded "others" who were ostracized by the Pharisees and their teachers of the Law. These outsiders ate together, banding together out of necessity; the Pharisees were scrupulous about how they ate; they were scrupulous about who they ate with.

Jesus came to call sinners to repentance, even sinners that others viewed as being beyond the reach of salvation. Levi and his friends were of concern to Jesus, as were all others. His call for all to come was expected; that is what a Savior does. Doctors treat sick people; they don't avoid them and tell them to go away. And neither did Jesus tell *all* who were (are) spiritually sick to go away. The Great Physician was interested in all His patients. He alone was the cure they needed. When Jesus reached out to lepers, tax collectors, women, and Gentiles, He was appealing to those on the margins of society. They were not "good enough" for salvation. They needed to change before they came to the kingdom; they needed to get all cleaned up, make themselves presentable, and then, maybe only then, would the religious establishment allow them in.

Here is perhaps the rub for folks today: We might have a hard time ever admitting that we are sick. Recognizing our sickness means that we cannot, by ourselves, get better. This is not what we want to hear; this violates our self-sufficiency and pride; we don't need anyone. This attitude is certainly part of our 21st century individualistic way of thinking. But is it also *not* the way Jesus presents Himself and His saving gospel? Jesus invites all to come to Him; many, then, did come to the kingdom. But why do we need a king and kingdom today? Why don't we seek a spiritual cure? Because we are not sick. We are dying and don't know it. So, we don't come to Jesus.

CHAPTER 9

Lord of the Sabbath

"Now it happened that He was passing through some grain fields on a Sabbath; and His disciples were picking the heads of grain, rubbing them in their hands, and eating the grain. But some of the Pharisees said, 'Why do you do what is not lawful on the Sabbath?' And Jesus answering them said, 'Have you not even read what David did when he was hungry, he and those who were with him, how he entered the house of God, and took and ate the consecrated bread which is not lawful for any to eat except the priests alone, and gave it to his companions?' And He was saying to them, 'The Son of Man is Lord of the Sabbath.'"

(Luke 6:1-5)

The initial popularity Jesus enjoyed at the beginning of His Galilean ministry is now waning. The Pharisees were always watching (Luke 5:17); they questioned His credentials (Luke 5:21); and Jesus' parables make it clear that His kingdom was not going to be the kind of kingdom the Jews expected. Now, He amps up the tension by supposedly violating the Sabbath day (He didn't; John 8:46). Observance of the Sabbath was one of the Ten Commandments. Countless arguments about what constituted work on the Sabbath only elevated their heated debates. Why would Jesus allow and participate in "picking" and "rubbing" and "eating" the grain found in the fields? He answered by appealing to scripture; if this is what David did, why would the Pharisees now try to catch Jesus in doing wrong? The priests allowed David to eat some of the consecrated bread used in the tabernacle; normally, the bread was reserved for the priests (1 Samuel 21:1-6). When the bread was replaced each week, the old bread could then be eaten by the priests (see Leviticus 24).

The priests were to prepare bread each week and arrange it accordingly in the tabernacle. And they were to provide oil for the lamps. By doing what the Lord commanded, they were obeying the Lord. More, though, they were acknowledging that the Lord was there with them: the bread of the Presence. Exodus 25:30: "You shall set the bread of the Presence on the table before Me at all times." The oil and the bread reminded Israel that they depended on God for who they were and for what they had. Gathering olives for oil and wheat for bread was possible because of God's blessings.

Now Jesus says, "I am Lord of the Sabbath." This claim arrays Jesus against the Jews who were so scrupulous and careful about Sabbath Day keeping and about maintaining the purity of the Temple. If David could do what he did, how much more could Jesus, the Lord of David, do what He did (Luke 20:41-44)? I am here. I am before you. I invite you to be part of My kingdom. The Sabbath was made for man. I am the Son of Man, Lord of all. Eating bread on the Sabbath points to the issue of authority. If Jesus is God's Son, then He could claim authority from heaven. Accepting what Jesus said about the Sabbath, or any other matter, indicates that one acknowledges Jesus as Lord. "Why do you call me Lord, Lord, and do not do what I say?" Will you call upon Jesus as your Lord? The Pharisees would not do that. In fact, they plotted to kill Jesus. But, after all, He did break the Sabbath.

CHAPTER 10

The Beatitudes

"Blessed are you when men hate you, and ostracize you, and insult you, and scorn your name as evil, for the sake of the Son of Man. Be glad in that day and leap for joy, for behold, your reward is great in heaven. For in the same way their fathers used to treat the prophets. Woe to you who are well-fed now, for you shall be hungry. Woe to you who laugh now, for you shall mourn and weep. Woe to you when all men speak well of you, for their fathers used to treat the false prophets in the same way."
(Luke 6:20-26 NASV)

Jesus' Sermon on the Mount turned the conventional values and wisdom of His day on their head. His beatitudes strike at the heart of first century values, systemic values that corroded the Law of Moses and God's chosen people. Jesus said to look deeper. Don't settle for the thinking of this world. There is more. Still, these same values, worldviews, and prejudices continue to corrode the lives and hearts of people today. Why? Could it be that we simply want a kingdom of our own?

"And turning His gaze toward His disciples, He began to say, 'Blessed are you who are poor, for yours is the kingdom of God.'" The stakes are raised. Who can be part of the kingdom? To whom does the kingdom belong? To the rich, the powerful, the religious guardians of conventional wisdom? No, the kingdom is for those who are blessed or find true happiness in being poor; the kingdom belongs to them. But weren't most of the people during Jesus' time poor? Yes. Being poor then is not necessarily being in abject poverty for the things of this life ("things" though, can get in the way of accepting Jesus). Kingdom people are poor in spirit; they recognize their spiritual poverty. They know that without Jesus and His kingdom they are paupers, even if they had amassed a fortune along the way. Jesus said, "But woe to you who are rich, for you are receiving your comfort in full." If this is how you live, if these are the things you want, then you already have your reward.

"Blessed are you who hunger now, for you shall be satisfied." How is your appetite? What fills your heart, your life? Spiritual people have spiritual appetites. Kingdom citizens yearn for, pursue, long for the riches of the teaching of Jesus, even when He demands much sacrifice. The insatiable thirst for God is a thirst that is never enough. How much of God do we want? Jesus fed the multitudes; they were hungry and were blessed with a good meal. They soon, though, refused His offer of food that would sustain them for eternity. Sadly, we do the same when we are satisfied with what we believe are truly great and lasting "things." Jesus said, "Woe to you who are full, for you shall hunger." You will always be hungry when you turn from the kingdom of Christ. The kingdom of Christ stands in contrast to the Roman Empire in the first century and in contrast to the kingdoms of the world today. Because we live in a social and political and economic context, our response to Jesus' invitation to be a part of His kingdom will have implications for our everyday walk through this world. The challenge remains: Seek first My kingdom! Will we do that?

CHAPTER 11

John the Baptist

"When the messengers of John had left, He began to speak to the crowds about John, 'What did you go out into the wilderness to see? A reed shaken by the wind? But what did you go out to see? A man dressed in soft clothing? Those who are splendidly clothed and live in luxury are found in royal palaces! But what did you go out to see? A prophet? Yes, I say to you, and one who is more than a prophet. This is the one about whom it is written, Behold, I send My messenger ahead of You, who will prepare Your way before You. I say to you, among those born of women there is no one greater than John; yet he who is least in the kingdom of God is greater than he.'"
(Luke 7:24-28 NASV)

Jesus, in the minds of many, did not act as a Messiah, a Deliverer. True, His kingdom was a kingdom of peace—peace between God and man, though, not peace among nations, or peace among two groups of people who hated each other—the Jews and the Gentiles. Add to the mix the thumb of Roman domination, and the first century was ripe for turmoil. Jesus didn't answer the call of the Jews to sit on an earthly throne (John 6:15); His rule of the universe was inward. He called for changed hearts among all who accepted His invitation (Matthew 11:28-30). What about John the Baptist? John was the messenger sent by the Lord. Jewish familiarity with the Old Testament should have whetted their appetites for his advent; John's message about someone greater to come should have stirred greater interest in his message. For some it did. John ended up in Herod's prison because of the truth he had preached. John certainly had the courage of his convictions. What were the people expecting when they went to see John in the wilderness? Would they meet a soft-spoken man in soft raiment? Would they find someone who was living a life of luxury or sacrifice? Would his message be palatable? If the Jews listened carefully, they could know that John was preparing them for the coming of someone greater. The Shekinah went before Israel as they left Egypt; John went before, ahead of Jesus, and preached a message of repentance—the One to come expects this of you if you want His kingdom. Get ready John says!

John was a great man; Jesus said so. But what of those who would come after John and be part of Jesus' kingdom? The Old Testament prophets anticipated something greater than the old confines of Judaism. "For truly I say to you that many prophets and righteous men desired to see what you see, and did not see it, and to hear what you hear, and did not hear it" (Matthew 13:7). These faithful men of old set forth God's intent to bring peace and salvation to all. "As to this salvation, the prophets who prophesied of the grace that would come to you made careful searches and inquiries, seeking to know what person or time the Spirit of Christ within them was indicating as He predicted the sufferings of Christ and the glories to follow. It was revealed to them that they were not serving themselves, but you, in these things which now have been announced to you through those who preached the gospel to you by the Holy Spirit sent from heaven—things into which angels long to see" (1 Peter 1:10-12). What they longed for is here for all, now. The least among men are great before God in His kingdom. A new day has dawned; a new status is available. We can be greater than the prophets and John. Because of what we have or because of who we are? No! The Messiah says come; that is what makes the difference.

CHAPTER 12

The Woman Sinner

"Now one of the Pharisees was requesting Him to dine with him, and He entered the Pharisee's house and reclined at the table. And there was a woman in the city who was a sinner; and when she learned that He was reclining at the table in the Pharisee's house, she brought an alabaster vial of perfume, and standing behind Him at His feet, weeping, she began to wet His feet with her tears, and kept wiping them with the hair of her head, and kissing His feet and anointing them with the perfume. Now when the Pharisee who had invited Him saw this, he said to himself, 'If this man were a prophet, He would know who and what sort of person this woman is who is touching Him, that she is a sinner.'"
(Luke 7:36-39)

Mary's hymn (Luke 1:46-55) said the Messiah would bring down "rulers from their thrones, exalt those who were humble and fill the hungry with good things" and send "away the rich empty-handed?" (1:52-53). Jesus preached the gospel to the poor (Luke 7:22). He healed the sick; He fed the hungry. He did for others what they could not do for themselves. But the help Jesus gives illustrates what kind of people we need to be in order to be in His kingdom. The centurion with a sick servant, the widow with a dead son, and the woman sinner were poor people. Were they in abject poverty? Maybe or maybe not. They did recognize that only Jesus could fill their need. They came to Jesus in faith, trusting Him. That is the only thing poor people can do; that is the only thing that brings about restoration. To their credit the Gentile, the widow, and the woman sinner realized their condition.

Jesus was dining in the home of a Pharisee. Evidently the woman who came and anointed Jesus' feet was well-known in "the city." Was she a woman of the "night?" Luke doesn't say. But she did have a reputation as a sinner. How could she walk into the party? Evidence from the first century tells us that her actions were not uncommon; when a well-known teacher was present in someone's house, outsiders might linger at the doorway in order to listen or to acknowledge the greatness of the honored guest. The greater concern was the fact that she approached Jesus and made contact with Him.

The woman sinner used costly perfume to anoint Jesus' feet. The cost of the oil was great. Besides the oil were her tears—tears of joy, thankfulness, contrition; she kissed Jesus' feet. Her actions aroused ire and suspicion among the seated guests; Simon the Pharisee is exposed. If Jesus was really a prophet, He would have known who this woman was. Jesus then teaches again about being poor. There was a creditor with two debtors, one owing lots of money, the other a smaller sum. Both were forgiven. Which debtor loved his benefactor the most? "I suppose the one whom he forgave the most." That was the right answer.

How much do we love Jesus? Just a little bit? Are we overwhelmed with thankfulness and tears and expressions of contrition because of our spiritual poverty? Do we know we will always be poor without Jesus? Great forgiveness should result in great love. The woman provided all the right responses in coming to Jesus that Simon failed to provide. Love, contrition, tears, a costly gift—all with no expectation—only the joy of being with Jesus—that was enough. He is always enough.

CHAPTER 13

Women in the Kingdom

"Soon afterwards, He began going around from one city and village to another, proclaiming and preaching the kingdom of God. The twelve were with Him, and also some women who had been healed of evil spirits and sicknesses: Mary who was called Magdalene, from whom seven demons had gone out, and Joanna the wife of Chuza, Herod's steward, and Susanna, and many others who were contributing to their support out of their private means."
(Luke 8:1-3 NASV)

At this point in Luke's narrative, Jesus was continuing to preach the kingdom of God. The gospel, the good news, includes the kingdom; but what does that mean? The Roman centurion found out something about the kingdom when Jesus healed the soldier's sick servant; the faith of the centurion would be necessary in order to be part of the kingdom. The woman sinner who came in tears, contrition, and repentance left with forgiveness. Isn't that a part of the kingdom? The kingdom of God, the rule of God, the giving over of one's complete self to the Master—is expressed in numerous ways by Jesus, by His works, His power, His compassion—all in an effort to draw men and women to the true meaning of what it means to be kingdom citizens. What Jesus said about the kingdom and about His role as the Messiah was out of kilter with 1st century religious, conventional wisdom. His kingdom was spiritual; He did not depend on soldiers and swords in order to grow the kingdom. Instead, He appealed to hearts of faith—to those who would yield to His reign in their lives. Now, Luke tells us that several women were also following Jesus; they were interested in the kingdom; they helped promote the kingdom by providing daily necessities. This was revolutionary. Luke mentions women throughout his narrative (1:5; 2:36; 7:36; 10:38; 13:10; 15:8; 18:1). Many men in the first century said that women were not to be seen or heard. Some men rejoiced that they had not been born as women. In our egalitarian world, these attitudes are offensive and wrong. That doesn't change history, though.

Can we see that Jesus, by inviting and including faithful women in His work, was recognizing their equal status before God? Whatever the service and work was, women and men are equal spiritually before God. "There is neither Jew nor Greek, there is neither slave nor free man, there is neither male nor female; for you are all one in Christ Jesus. And if you belong to Christ, then you are Abraham's descendants, heirs according to promise" (Galatians 3:28-29).

What about these women mentioned by Luke? Mary Magdalene had seven demons cast out of her. Her disreputable reputation came into being long after the first century; there is no New Testament evidence about any kind of immorality on her part. Joanna was the wife of Chuza, a first century political figure. We know nothing more about Susanna. But there were others who also helped in the material sustaining of Jesus and His disciples as they went about preaching the good news of the kingdom. These women were willing to share and follow and learn. They were a part of Christ's kingdom, weren't they? There is room in the kingdom for all, men and women, isn't there? Do you want to be in the greatest kingdom this world shall ever know? Then follow Jesus.

CHAPTER 14

The Transfiguration

"Some eight days after these sayings, He took along Peter and John and James, and went up on the mountain to pray. And while He was praying, the appearance of His face became different, and His clothing became white and gleaming. And behold, two men were talking with Him; and they were Moses and Elijah, who, appearing in glory, were speaking of His departure which He was about to accomplish at Jerusalem. Now Peter and his companions had been overcome with sleep; but when they were fully awake, they saw His glory and the two men standing with Him. And as these were leaving Him, Peter said to Jesus, Master, it is good for us to be here; let us make three tabernacles: one for You, and one for Moses, and one for Elijah—not realizing what he was saying. While he was saying this, a cloud formed and began to overshadow them; and they were afraid as they entered the cloud. Then a voice came out of the cloud, saying, This is My Son, My Chosen One; listen to Him! And when the voice had spoken, Jesus was found alone. And they kept silent, and reported to no one in those days any of the things which they had seen."
(Luke 9:28-36 NASV)

Peter, James, and John, three intimate disciples of Jesus, went up the mountain to pray. Imagine, if you can, the very thought of bowing before the Father above even as you are in the presence of the Father's only begotten Son! These three, while part of the larger group of followers, were included in the activities of Jesus in private, intimate ways. Can we extrapolate from these associations that these three were to be singled out for great things in the future? All three are mentioned prominently in the rest of the New Testament. The voice of the Father said, "This is My beloved Son, My Chosen One; listen to Him." This would have been startling; too, it would have also opened a window to who Jesus was (is). Hear Jesus, the Father says. Moses and Elijah are on the mount. The need to listen to Jesus now takes precedence over the Law that would be nailed to the cross and over the prophets, as they yielded to the greatest prophet of all. The Father said that Jesus is "My Son." Ancient kings of Israel were called the sons of God. Jesus is the royal Son as depicted in the Psalms. "I have installed my king on Zion, my holy mountain. I will proclaim the Lord's decree: He said to me, 'you are my son; today I have become your father,'" (Psalm 2:6-7). Jesus is the chosen one of the Father. Jesus is the servant of the Father. Jesus' role as Servant meant that He would suffer and die on the cross for the sins of the world. "Behold, My Servant, whom I uphold; My chosen one in whom My soul delights. I have put My Spirit upon Him; He will bring forth justice to the nations. He will not cry out or raise His voice" (Isaiah 42:1; 53).

When Peter suggested building three tents for Moses, Elijah, and Jesus, his intention might have been a good one. Did he want to prolong this magnificent occasion; we can camp and stay for a long time? Whatever his motivation, Luke says that Peter didn't realize what he was saying. And that is what happens to us. We don't understand, we don't listen, we don't know what to do. The only solution, the best solution, is to listen to the Father declare His love for His Son. The brightness, the brilliance, the transforming of Jesus' image portends the ultimate victory of Jesus over Satan, over sin, over temptation, over death. We can hardly look and take it all in. But we must try. Where else can we look?

CHAPTER 15

What Must I Do to Inherit Eternal Life?

"And a lawyer stood up and put Him to the test, saying, 'Teacher, what shall I do to inherit eternal life?' And He said to him, 'What is written in the Law? How does it read to you?' And he answered, 'You shall love the Lord your God with all your heart, and with all your soul, and with all your strength, and with all your mind; and your neighbor as yourself.' And He said to him, 'You have answered correctly; do this and you will live.' But wishing to justify himself, he said to Jesus, 'And who is my neighbor?'"
(Luke 10:25-29 NASV; note vv. 30-37, the Parable of the Good Samaritan that illustrates who one's neighbor might be)

A Jewish lawyer, one trained in the nuances of the Law of Moses, asked a good question. How do we reach the worthy goal of eternal life? Jesus spoke about a life of faith while on this earth, and everlasting life in the world to come (John 20:30-31). A life of faith is a life lived, an active life. The inheritance of eternal life would be the grandest of all. Did the lawyer want to live a life of faith; or, did he simply want eternal life—something to be gained but not actually lived out in daily practice? Can you separate the two? But still, the lawyer was a believer in God; he knew something about God and about God's will. For this we might give him credit for his question. Luke, though, exposes the lawyer's real motive; he was putting Jesus to the test.

Jesus engaged in Bible study with the lawyer. You have asked a question; you know the Law; how does what you already know answer your question?

The lawyer quoted Deuteronomy 6:5, the Great Commandment. Now the test will come. Was the lawyer willing to give himself in total dedication to God and His commandments? Surely, he answered yes! Would he extend that same love and concern to an outsider? Or, would he remain entrenched in a narrow view of who could actually be included in the kingdom? Could a Samaritan be a candidate for kingdom citizenship? Loving God is essential to eternal life; so is loving the right people, even those you don't necessarily want to love. We want to love the neighbors we want to love; others we are not so sure about.

The Good Samaritan is a familiar story. Sermons, lessons, and Bible readings have elevated the Good Samaritan to a status of acceptability that was not the case in the first century. When Jesus said the Good Samaritan helped a man who had been beaten by robbers, the lawyer's credulity was stretched. The non-actions of the priest and Levite, two men who knew something about the Law, only added to the lawyer's prejudice; after all, he was in league with these *religious* men. The lawyer was culpable, too. Are you hoping that some people turn out not to be your neighbor? Do you dread having to stop and help? Are you more comfortable passing by on the other side? Are you afraid that stopping might cost you something? Could someone you think to be an enemy of God might actually be someone who loves God and also loves others? Jesus asked: Of the three men in the story, which one was a neighbor to the wounded man left by the roadside? The lawyer answered: The one who showed mercy toward him. Was he afraid to even utter the word *Samaritan*? Are we?

CHAPTER 16

A House Divided

"And He was casting out a demon, and it was mute; when the demon had gone out, the mute man spoke; and the crowds were amazed. But some of them said, He casts out demons by Beelzebul, the ruler of the demons. Others, to test Him, were demanding of Him a sign from heaven. But He knew their thoughts and said to them, Any kingdom divided against itself is laid waste; and a house divided against itself falls. If Satan also is divided against himself, how will his kingdom stand? For you say that I cast out demons by Beelzebul. And if I by Beelzebul cast out demons, by whom do your sons cast them out? So, they will be your judges. But if I cast out demons by the finger of God, then the kingdom of God has come upon you."
(Luke 11:14-20 NASV)

Opposition to Jesus is growing. The religious leaders continued to question His authority. Who gave you the right to teach and act as You are doing? To discredit Jesus, they attributed His ability to work miracles to Beelzebul. The people were amazed that a man who could not speak now spoke. Beelzebul is thought to be associated with the Philistine god Ekron. "Now Moab rebelled against Israel after the death of Ahab. And Ahaziah fell through the lattice in his upper chamber which was in Samaria, and became ill. So he sent messengers and said to them, 'Go, inquire of Baal-zebub, the god of Ekron, whether I will recover from this sickness'" (2 Kings 1:1-2). The name was not complementary; the people were trying to link Jesus to Satan. Others asked for another sign, continuing to put Jesus to the test. They did not doubt Jesus' ability to work miracles; to question such power would be a rejection of Jesus as God's

Son. Is that their concern? Remember that Jesus is preaching the gospel of the kingdom. If He is in league with Satan, if He cast out demons by the power of Beelzebul, how can Satan's kingdom stand? Divided kingdoms cannot stand. The Jews claimed to have exorcists—those who cast out demons; where did they get their power? Were they legitimate, or did they depend on Satan to do their work?

Jesus said: But if I cast out demons by the finger of God, then the kingdom of God has come upon you. Jesus' miracles were evidence of the arrival of the kingdom. The time had come; the Messiah was present; the power of God was being demonstrated; all were invited to yield their hearts and lives. Here are the miracles; here is God's power; it is obvious and singular. God does not depend upon Satan to accomplish His will. When Jesus died on the cross, Satan's power was broken. Rival kingdoms exist; the demise of Satan's kingdom was assured when Jesus came and died. Don't make the mistake of choosing the wrong kingdom, the wrong savior, the wrong master. Jesus, the strong man, entered into the house of Satan; after three days Jesus emerged victorious. Make the right choice. A house divided will not stand.

"For the kingdom of God does not consist in words but in power" (1 Corinthians 4:20). "For the kingdom of God is not eating and drinking, but righteousness and peace and joy in the Holy Spirit" (Romans 14:17). "Put on the full armor of God, so that you will be able to stand firm against the schemes of the devil" (Ephesians 6:11). Are we with Jesus? Or, are we against Him?

CHAPTER 17

The Sign of Jonah

> "As the crowds were increasing, He began to say, 'This generation is a wicked generation; it seeks for a sign, and yet no sign will be given to it but the sign of Jonah. For just as Jonah became a sign to the Ninevites, so will the Son of Man be to this generation. The Queen of the South will rise up with the men of this generation at the judgment and condemn them, because she came from the ends of the earth to hear the wisdom of Solomon; and behold, something greater than Solomon is here. The men of Nineveh will stand up with this generation at the judgment and condemn it, because they repented at the preaching of Jonah; and behold, something greater than Jonah is here."
> (Luke 11:29-32 NASV)

When asked about where His power to work miracles came from, Jesus said, "But if I cast out demons by the finger of God, then the kingdom of God has come upon you" (Luke 11:20). The advent of the Holy Spirit of God meant the inauguration of the kingdom; the inbreaking of God's rule over His creation had begun. The Old Testament prophets spoke of the coming of the Spirit and the establishment of the Messianic kingdom (Isaiah 2; 61). Salvation was possible. Did the multitudes come to Jesus for salvation? What were their true intentions? Did they see the need to repent in order to be part of the kingdom? Jesus called them "a wicked generation." Jesus refused to satisfy their desire for another sign; all of the signs were never enough.

The sign of Jonah would be a sign for future generations. Jonah being thrown out of the ship into the water and then being swallowed by the great fish mirrors what happened to Jesus. Jesus was crucified, was buried, and was raised three days later. Jonah spent three days and nights in the belly of the fish. After reaching dry land, Jonah then went to Nineveh and preached God's message of repentance. After Jesus came forth from the grave, His message rang forth into all the world. Why should those who heard the gospel believe and obey? Because Jesus is alive! He was raised from the grave! He rules and reigns!

Again, though, could those who continued to ask for signs ever know God's truth and obey and be saved? If so, how? They needed to do what the people of Nineveh did; the people of Nineveh listened to Jonah's preaching, believed, and obeyed. Why were they saved? Because they repented at the preaching of the gospel. Why should the sign seekers do the same? Because something greater was at work. The preaching of Jonah was God's sign to Nineveh; it was enough to convince honest hearts to come to repentance. Today, the preaching of the gospel is God's sign that He wants all to listen, believe, and repent. Is this a miraculous sign like those Jesus performed? No. But it is an adequate sign. The gospel is enough because Jesus was raised from the dead. Jonah's actions anticipated the ultimate expression of salvation realized in Jesus' gospel.

Are you seeking some kind of sign from God before you decide to obey His gospel? Be careful. If you won't accept the gospel, neither will you accept a sign. For you, any sign and the gospel are not enough. "He said, 'Oh no, father Abraham, but if someone from the dead goes to them, they will repent.' Then Abraham said, 'If they will not listen to Moses and the prophets, neither will they be persuaded if someone should rise from the dead'" (Luke 16:30-31).

CHAPTER 18

Woe on the Pharisees

"But woe to you Pharisees! For you pay tithe of mint and rue and every kind of garden herb, and yet disregard justice and the love of God; but these are the things you should have done without neglecting the others. Woe to you Pharisees! For you love the chief seats in the synagogues and the respectful greetings in the market places. Woe to you! For you are like concealed tombs, and the people who walk over them are unaware of it."
(Luke 11:42-44 NASV)

Interestingly, Luke often casts the activities and teachings of Jesus in the context of a meal. In Luke 11, Jesus accepted the invitation for lunch in the home of a Pharisee. The table was set; the food was ready; but Jesus didn't wash his hands before eating, an omission the host notices. While the Pharisee didn't say anything, Jesus knew about him and his Pharisaical insistence on ceremonial purity. Jesus also was concerned about neglected hearts. With great grief at their pretense of religion, Jesus delivered six woes that called out their hypocrisy.

No one enjoys eating food from dishes that appear to be clean, on the outside anyway, and then getting to the end of the bowl or cup, only to find grime and leftover food. The picture is disgusting. Great care is shown for the outside; the inside is neglected. The outside should not be overlooked; vessels should be clean (Leviticus 11:32-33). Jesus' greater concern is the heart. A heart full of robbery and wickedness cannot make the outside clean. Immorality and taking advantage of others indicate a heart that needs cleansing. Jesus says give alms to the poor—show concern for others—this is the kind of heart you need. Tithing or giving a tenth of one's goods comes from Old Testament practices. What good is a tenth if you lack love and mercy? Pride drives people to the best seats in the synagogue. You may sit at the head table, but your pride means more than Jesus does. The Pharisees, so concerned about purity, were walking over graves—graves, symbols of death and uncleanness; these were the hallmarks of their religion rather than true, heartfelt religion. Still, the outside looked OK.

Jesus' wide net insulted a lawyer (scribe). Would all of the religious establishment face Jesus' ire? Yes, because they all needed to repent. Jesus told the scribe to stop insisting that others do what he himself was unwilling to do. While the burdens of the Pharisees (a ship's heavy cargo) might reflect a true interest in being right with the Lord, they were actually unwilling to show true mercy and concern even for their fellow Jews—those who might have been concerned about doing God's will.

The Pharisees teach us this lesson: We can maintain the outward appearance of religion, that is, the outside of the cup looks clean and useful, but in reality, our professions of piety and devotion are empty—empty words and shams. The only way to get the inside of the cup clean is to change the heart. While we are doing that, let us remember that religion practiced *outwardly only* for too long a time can lead to hypocrisy. Does that insult you? Then talk to the scribe. Better, talk to Jesus.

CHAPTER 19

Bigger Barns

"Someone in the crowd said to Him, 'Teacher, tell my brother to divide the family inheritance with me.' But He said to him, 'Man, who appointed Me a judge or arbitrator over you?' Then He said to them, 'Beware, and be on your guard against every form of greed; for not even when one has an abundance does his life consist of his possessions.' And He told them a parable, saying, 'the land of a rich man was very productive. And he began reasoning to himself, saying, 'what shall I do, since I have no place to store my crops?' Then he said, 'this is what I will do: I will tear down my barns and build larger ones, and there I will store all my grain and my goods. And I will say to my soul, Soul, you have many goods laid up for many years to come; take your ease, eat, drink and be merry.' But God said to him, 'you fool! This very night your soul is required of you; and now who will own what you have prepared?' So is the man who stores up treasure for himself, and is not rich toward God."
(Luke 12:13-21 NASV)

The judgment Jesus brought went beyond the daily, ordinary affairs of life. For example, there are greater issues to think about rather than squabbling over money and inheritances. Jesus is trying to help us understand that true living reaches beyond the accumulations of land, money, and prestige. If we are only concerned about our "share" of whatever, then we are headed in the wrong direction; we are straying farther from the kingdom of heaven. Since the things of this life pertain to this life, and because the things of this life perish, then our concentration needs to be on the life to come, the true life that lasts for eternity.

The things of this life do not necessarily have to present dangers to us. We can work hard, be successful, use what we have to help others. Still, we must recognize that everything comes from God. The dangers and traps come when we pursue bigger barns. Bigger barns can be distractions. The desire for more and more is a sign of covetousness. "Covetousness is idolatry" (Colossians 3:5). More will not satisfy. "He who loves money will not be satisfied with money, nor he who loves abundance with its income. This too is vanity" (Ecclesiastes 5:10). When we are growing more crops and building bigger barns, we have little time left for spiritual growth. Have we become idolaters? Scripture warns about the dangers of greed. We are living "bumper crop" lives. We are blessed and yet, we must always be careful. One danger is that we could end up hating our brother because he got part of our inheritance.

Notice in our passage the small words "my" and "I." "My" and "I" may lead to a good retirement; do they lead to heaven? We are rich, but what direction have our riches taken us? Ultimately, what do we really need to sustain life here on earth? Actually, very little. Jesus said that if we have some food to eat, clothes to wear, and a place to live, then we have what we need. If bigger barns come our way, let us use them to the Lord's glory. Let's remember, though, that we will not find safety in those bigger barns when we stand before Christ in judgment.

CHAPTER 20

Christ the Divider

"I have come to cast fire upon the earth; and how I wish it were already kindled! But I have a baptism to undergo, and how distressed I am until it is accomplished! Do you suppose that I came to grant peace on earth? I tell you, no, but rather division; for from now on five members in one household will be divided, three against two and two against three. They will be divided, father against son and son against father, mother against daughter and daughter against mother, mother-in-law against daughter-in-law and daughter-in-law against mother-in-law."
(Luke 12:49-53 NASV)

It is impossible to remain neutral about Jesus—about who He is and what He demands of all who decide to follow Him. Jesus is not simply one way among many; He is **the** Way, **the** Truth, and **the** Life (John 14:6). His way is narrow and hard. His way places His followers in opposition to those who find His call to be difficult and repulsive. If you decide to follow Jesus you might encounter alienation, turmoil, and even hatred. Sadly, you might find your own family turning from you and your newfound faith. Yet, we shouldn't be surprised; Jesus came to bring division.

Luke refers to Jesus' "mission statement" with the words "I have come to..." Jesus came to do many things. For example, He came to bring the fire of judgment, a recurring theme in Luke's gospel. "Indeed, the axe is already laid at the root of the trees; so, every tree that does not bear good fruit is cut down and thrown into the fire" (3:9). Judgment had already begun. Jesus' baptism points to His own death on the cross. He is distressed about the cross; it was for this purpose that He came into the world. He was ready to accomplish the Father's will that would bring salvation to all mankind. Jesus was rejected and persecuted; He was accursed by hanging on a tree (Acts 5:30). In dying, Jesus bore the judgment of sin for the world.

Anyone who decided to follow Jesus to the cross, needed to know that they could be opposed by their loved ones. This was serious, especially in a culture of family relationships, clans, ancestries, and social ties. No one wanted to be separated from their family. In fact, first century families were extended families; lots of relatives lived together because of hard economic necessity. Jesus said this would happen; don't be surprised; this goes with the territory of following Him. "For son treats father contemptuously, daughter rises up against her mother, daughter-in-law against her mother-in-law; A man's enemies are the men of his own household" (Micah 7:6). Who is in the household of Jesus? Those who do His will.

Jesus said to "read" the signs of the times (Luke 12:54). His challenge, even now, is to discern correctly, evaluate honestly, and probe deeply concerning the kingdom—a kingdom that is not of this world. Count the cost before you jump in headfirst. How many do not count the cost? How many were infused with initial fervor, only to soon let the fire go out? Remember that our own culture increasingly challenges the very notion of absolute truth, a standard of morality that applies to all, and resists the temerity of saying that someone is wrong. Take a stand for truth and for Jesus and you will be divided from most. Your loved ones may be standing against you. True peace is possible; but it comes with a price. Are we willing to pay that price? Jesus was.

CHAPTER 21

Repentance

"Now on the same occasion there were some present who reported to Him about the Galileans whose blood Pilate had mixed with their sacrifices. And Jesus said to them, do you suppose that these Galileans were greater sinners than all other Galileans because they suffered this fate? I tell you, no, but unless you repent, you will all likewise perish."
(read Luke 13:1-9 NASV)

Tragedies, either deliberate or by accident, generally pique the interest of those who were involved in the episode; or, some just wanted to talk about what had happened. Some came to Jesus, talking about Pilate killing some Galileans and mixing bloody sacrifices. Where and when did this happen? No one knows. Then, a tower in Siloam fell, killing eighteen men. Jewish thinking in the first century blamed the sins of those who had been killed; if trouble came to those involved, then it must have been because they had in some manner violated God's will. Did Rome really have the right to go around killing people? Would Jesus take sides in these matters? Did He even care about these events and the personal trauma that came to those involved? Jesus' call to repent was meant to force His listeners to focus on their own lives and on their own relationship with God. The Galileans and those killed by the falling tower were dead; they could not be brought back; they could no longer serve God and repent. Maybe they needed to repent; maybe they did; we don't know. That is not the point. Those who listened to Jesus could repent. They could follow Jesus and become part of His kingdom. Repentance had been the constant cry of John the Baptist and of Jesus. The tragic death is when the deceased leaves this world unprepared for judgment. A tragic death can only be averted now, in this life, by following the Lord. Sin is associated with death; sin brings death; we must face our mortality. Disaster always follows a failure to repent.

You may have an accident and lose your life; this may be through no fault of your own. You may make certain choices (bad, good, neutral) that may end your life. The point is: When will these things happen? Do you know? We must be prepared to leave this old world at any time. The problem is that we continue to live not thinking about what Pilate might do to us or about a tower falling on us. When something happens to someone else, we take some notice. But until we repent, we really haven't been serious about truly following Jesus. We haven't noticed anything at all.

Death is coming to all. The only thing that will make a difference in your life at that time is repentance. Repent or not, you are going to die. Repent or not, a tower might fall on you. Repent or not, an accident might take your life. It is not when we will die; it is that we will die. That is the value of Jesus' call to repent. He wants us to be ready to meet Him on the last day. What about the Galileans and those killed by the tower? What about their spiritual condition? We don't know. The question is: What about yours?

CHAPTER 22

Invited Guests

"And He also went on to say to the one who had invited Him, when you give a luncheon or a dinner, do not invite your friends or your brothers or your relatives or rich neighbors, otherwise they may also invite you in return and that will be your repayment. But when you give a reception, invite the poor, the crippled, the lame, the blind, and you will be blessed, since they do not have the means to repay you; for you will be repaid at the resurrection of the righteous."
(Luke 14:12-14 NASV)

At this point in His earthly ministry, Jesus was closing out nearly three years of teaching and controversy. He had invited all, whether Jew and Gentile, to follow Him. How do we answer that call? Jesus was in the home of a Pharisee on the Sabbath. However, the invitation to sit and eat was a ruse to watch Jesus in order to catch Him in some compromise of the Law.

It is probably true of most of us that when we have guests into our homes, we invite people we know; they are mostly people like we are in terms of background, education, economic level, similar interests, and even in religious inclinations. To put it another way, how often do we find ourselves associating with complete strangers? How often do we make an effort to include those *dreaded others* into our supposed circle of influence? Who would even think about including people who could do absolutely nothing for us, save for coming to the table we prepared? Don't we really want prominent people to come to our table?

The guest with the highest honor would be seated on a couch at the head of the table; accordingly, other guests would take their expected seats around the head table; these seats were often determined by the host. If not, as an early arriving guest you could position yourself at the head table. After all, you are important, you deserve to be there, and tough luck to those who arrived late. How embarrassing, though, if the host told you to move to the back! "Do not claim honor in the presence of the king, and do not stand in the place of great men; for it is better that it be said to you, Come up here, than for you to be placed lower in the presence of the prince, whom your eyes have seen" (Proverbs 25:6-7).

Again, how do we answer Jesus' call to His kingdom? Pride, self-exaltation, and the desire for prestige and recognition are obstacles to having a true heart and desire for the things of Jesus. When we look for the chief seats, we say that we are more important than others; especially are we more important than those we consider to be below our station in life. We should be elevated, not them. When we focus on ourselves, we cannot see Jesus. How do we show humility and concern for others? Jesus said to invite others with no thought of what your guests can do for you. When we do that, we are following Jesus.

After all, isn't that what Jesus does? He invites us; we can come; we come in humility, in thankfulness, in a spirit of abject spiritual poverty. Jesus' invitation is for those who are more than happy to sit in the back of the building. We must not rush to the head table.

CHAPTER 23

The Prodigal Son

"And He said, 'A man had two sons.'"
(Luke 15:11 NASV)

Losing something dear to your heart makes you sad. You lament your loss; you start doing whatever is possible to do in order to find the lost item. When you find what you have lost, sadness turns into joy. Three stories in Luke 15 tell us that what is lost can be found; sadness can turn to rejoicing. And amazingly, we can rejoice along with our Father in heaven, our Savior, and the angels.

The loss of a sheep is great. The animal may be lost forever; the economic loss is significant. No faithful shepherd will stand idly by and watch an animal wander off into danger. Shepherd and sheep language were used by Old Testament prophets to illustrate our Creator's concern for His creation, His sheep. "Like a shepherd He will tend His flock, In His arm He will gather the lambs and carry them in His bosom; He will gently lead the nursing ewes" (Isaiah 40:11; cf. Ezekiel 34; Psalm 23). The spiritual connection to Jesus, the Good Shepherd, is obvious and important.

The father in Luke 15 had two sons; while the emphasis is on the younger, profligate son, the older son's attitudes and actions teach us, too. Sadly, the rebellious son mirrors the actions of countless millions; most of us know a son or daughter, a spouse, or close friend, who decided to journey into the alluring city of sin. And like the father in the story, we, too, stand every day watching, listening, and praying for even the slightest inclination that our loved one is on the way home.

Average workers in the first century could not afford to lose money. To lose even one drachma (equal to a denarius), a day's wage, was serious. Where is the lost coin? Is it close by? Using a light to carefully search the house, the lost coin was found; rejoicing ensued. Not only is the woman relieved; she wants her friends to rejoice with her. The effort expended was worth it. And so, it is with any and all who wander away from God. It takes effort to find the sheep and the coin. But what about the lost boy?

The younger son said, "Give me what is mine. I'm ready to leave home." And he did leave, making his foray into the pig pen of sin and ruin. Oh, the fun he had, at least at first. But then his money runs out, his friends run off, and now this young Jewish boy eats with the hogs. But, to his everlasting credit, he woke up. "I will get up and go to my father, and will say to him, Father, I have sinned against heaven, and in your sight." Who was looking for him? His father. In humility and confession, he returns home saying: I am willing to be a slave. No, you are my son, the father responds. It is time to rejoice and celebrate.

When we *come to ourselves and repent*, our status changes. We are no longer in ruin; destitution gives way to a better destiny. No longer do we live with strangers. We are again part of our true family; we have joined with our true Father and Savior. Our fortunes have been reversed. That is the hope Jesus gives us. That is why He came and lived and died and was raised. He gives hope to tax collectors, sinners, young sons, older sons, and daughters. He gives hope to you and me. Thank God, we are no longer lost; we have been found.

CHAPTER 24

Faithful in Little or Much

"He who is faithful in a very little thing is faithful also in much; and he who is unrighteous in a very little thing is unrighteous also in much. Therefore, if you have not been faithful in the use of unrighteous wealth, who will entrust the true riches to you? And if you have not been faithful in the use of that which is another's, who will give you that which is your own? No servant can serve two masters; for either he will hate the one and love the other, or else he will be devoted to one and despise the other. You cannot serve God and wealth."
(Luke 16:10-13 NASV)

Our use of wealth must be a constant concern as we strive to serve Jesus. The successful farmer turned out to be a fool; the rich man ended up in torments. Did wealth have something to do with their destiny? There is a danger in wealth, in riches, in success. "But those who want to get rich fall into temptation and a snare and many foolish and harmful desires which plunge men into ruin and destruction. For the love of money is a root of all sorts of evil, and some by longing for it have wandered away from the faith and pierced themselves with many griefs" (1 Timothy 6:9-10). On the other hand, we can use wisely what the Lord has entrusted to us; this should always be our aim (1 Corinthians 4:2). What was the aim of the unscrupulous servant? It seems that he was trying, even through dishonesty, to save his own neck. And, he was commended for his shrewdness. What are the lessons for us?

Jesus said the manager of goods that belonged to someone else acted with wisdom, with prudence. People in the world, do think about their wealth;

often their actions revolve around what they have and how to get more. Jesus followers must do the same in regard to spiritual wealth and blessings. We must wisely use the blessings of our relationship with the Lord; soon, we will be rewarded with eternal dwellings, an everlasting tabernacle that awaits the wise and spiritual. Do we use others for our own selfish good? No. But we can set good examples before the world by using wisely what God has given us? Do others see our willingness to share our wealth? Do they see our concern for each other and for those who have fallen by the wayside? Are we trustworthy in our handling of the little things that come to us? If we are careless in using our blessings, we cannot expect greater riches. The opposite will happen: What we have will be taken away. When our focus is mammon, we have already lost sight of the true riches of heaven. Serving two masters is impossible. Every choice contains at least an implicit acceptance or denial regarding the choices made.

Our money, our wealth can be and should be blessings to us and to others; in this, we glorify God. The problem with the pursuit of the things of this life is that we lose our focus on God. Our desire for more can distort the need we have for God. When we are successful, we say: Look at what we have done; we don't need anyone to help us. Attachment to this world detaches us from the world to come. What we have and how we use what we have has a lot to do with where we end up when this life is over. Let us hold loosely the things that perish; let us hold tightly to our Savior. Don't ever let go of Jesus.

CHAPTER 25

Ten Lepers

"While He was on the way to Jerusalem, He was passing between Samaria and Galilee. As He entered a village, ten leprous men who stood at a distance met Him; and they raised their voices, saying, Jesus, Master, have mercy on us! When He saw them, He said to them, Go and show yourselves to the priests. And as they were going, they were cleansed. Now one of them, when he saw that he had been healed, turned back, glorifying God with a loud voice, and he fell on his face at His feet, giving thanks to Him. And he was a Samaritan. Then Jesus answered and said, Were there not ten cleansed? But the nine—where are they? Was no one found who returned to give glory to God, except this foreigner? And He said to him, stand up and go; your faith has made you well."
(Luke 17:11-19 NASV)

Jesus continued marching toward Jerusalem; this inexorable determination is mentioned often by Luke (9:51; 13:22). As Jesus traveled from Galilee through Samaria, we are not surprised that He encountered a Samaritan. The Samaritans were viewed as outcasts by the Jews, this Samaritan was a leper—a double exclusion.

Lepers were excluded from society, forced to live apart from other people, and had to make sure no one came in contact with their uncleanness (Leviticus 13:45-46). These ten lepers were not in the village, but stood away from those who were coming and going. A cry for mercy to Jesus, the Master, the one who could actually help them, is not surprising; it is likely they knew something of Jesus and His work in helping others. The Law of Moses commanded that lepers be examined by the priests; this would ensure that the health of the lepers had actually been restored; then the lepers would give an offering in the temple in thanks for their cleansing. "But go and show yourself to the priest and make an offering for your cleansing, just as Moses commanded, as a testimony to them" (Luke 5:14).

Did the lepers need faith in order to do as Jesus commanded? The Lord said "go;" as they were going, they were cleansed, but not before they left to go. Luke says one leper, a Samaritan, returned to say *thank you*! Ten were cleansed; where are the nine? This Samaritan, this leper, this "foreigner" was the only one to return, fall on the ground, and give thanks for his healing. Ten were cleansed; one said thank you. In a leper colony, distinctions of ethnicity mattered little; their shared misery made them equal. Yet, the Jews would hardly believe that a Samaritan could do something of spiritual significance, even something as small as giving thanks. That fact that Jesus asked about the nine highlights their lack of thankfulness. Could that have been the real problem for the Jews? After all, they were the chosen people of God. They were the religious elite. Why should they bother saying thank you?

Here we are today. We are God's people. Do we down deep think we are better than everyone else? We have our salvation all wrapped up; it is secure; the Lord should be thanking us. Remember that Jesus said to the leper who returned: "Your faith has made you well." When Jesus says that to you and me, we need to run to Him as fast as possible, fall down, and say "thank you." And if we never get up again, that's OK.

CHAPTER 26

Pharisees and Publicans

"And He also told this parable to some people who trusted in themselves that they were righteous, and viewed others with contempt: Two men went up into the temple to pray, one a Pharisee and the other a tax collector. The Pharisee stood and was praying this to himself: 'God, I thank You that I am not like other people: swindlers, unjust, adulterers, or even like this tax collector. I fast twice a week; I pay tithes of all that I get.' But the tax collector, standing some distance away, was even unwilling to lift up his eyes to heaven, but was beating his breast, saying, 'God, be merciful to me, the sinner!' I tell you, this man went to his house justified rather than the other; for everyone who exalts himself will be humbled, but he who humbles himself will be exalted."
(Luke 18:9-14 NASV)

Jesus' target audience, the Pharisees, were those "who trusted in themselves." His disciples were close by, too, to hear Jesus contrast those who believed they didn't need God with those who knew their need. Who would question the spiritual status of the Pharisees? This particular Pharisee, pointed out all he had been doing in his religious life; he certainly tried to separate himself from the *dreaded others*, especially the tax collectors. Tax collectors were viewed as traitors; they worked for the despised Romans; they often cheated their own countrymen out of more money than was due. Why would Jesus use a tax collector to make His point? Why wouldn't He? Tax collectors, prostitutes, lepers—the dregs of society were the very ones Jesus came to save. Could Pharisees be saved? No doubt some were. But how? By their own righteousness? By their own good works? By their own perceptions of what kingdom living was all about? No, justification is possible only in a spirit of humility, not self-exaltation.

Praying to God is a good thing; it is needed; it is a blessing and privilege to speak with our heavenly Father. But how do we speak with Him? With boasting or humility? It is not that we shouldn't try to obey God's will; that is what the Pharisee did. But in his litany of religious expressions, the Pharisee saw himself as better than others; because of what he did, he thought he deserved the good will of God. The tax collector, however good or bad or notorious, knew he is a sinner. He beats his breast in contrition. He stands apart from the holy God he prayed to.

Is God's grace for all mankind? Yes! But what of those who don't see their undone, self-righteous condition before God? When humility eludes you, justification is impossible. Mercy comes to all who recognize that God alone is their only hope. The tax collector went home justified. The Pharisee went home, too. Was he thinking: Hey, no problem? All is well with my soul? What are you thinking?

CHAPTER 27

Zacchaeus

"He entered Jericho and was passing through. And there was a man called by the name of Zacchaeus; he was a chief tax collector and he was rich. Zacchaeus was trying to see who Jesus was, and was unable because of the crowd, for he was small in stature. So, he ran on ahead and climbed up into a sycamore tree in order to see Him, for He was about to pass through that way. When Jesus came to the place, He looked up and said to him, 'Zacchaeus, hurry and come down, for today I must stay at your house.' And he hurried and came down and received Him gladly. When they saw it, they all began to grumble, saying, 'He has gone to be the guest of a man who is a sinner.' Zacchaeus stopped and said to the Lord, 'Behold, Lord, half of my possessions I will give to the poor, and if I have defrauded anyone of anything, I will give back four times as much.' And Jesus said to him, 'Today, salvation has come to this house, because he, too, is a son of Abraham. For the Son of Man has come to seek and to save that which was lost.'"
(Luke 19:1-9 NASV)

Jesus said it was hard for rich people to enter into the kingdom (Luke 18:24). Yet, we can be thankful that God can, and does, bring wealthy people into the kingdom. Zacchaeus was an unlikely candidate for the kingdom from many standpoints; he was wealthy, he worked for the Roman government; he even had doubts about his past life. Now, Jesus goes home with him. The borders of the kingdom are broad.

Zacchaeus was interested in seeing Jesus; he climbed a tree to get a closer look. Jesus took the initiative, telling Zacchaeus to get down and then they would go home together. This wasn't the first time Jesus ate with tax collectors (Luke 5:27). "I must" stay at your house. It was a *necessity* for Jesus to go home with Zacchaeus. And why wouldn't Jesus do that? He came to seek and save the lost; even wealthy tax collectors were not beyond the pale of heaven's concern. Zacchaeus' neighbors didn't like what was happening; to them, he was a sinner. Zacchaeus realized the possibility that maybe he needed to right any wrongs committed in his tax work. He would give half of his goods (wealth) to the poor. He would repay to the max anyone he had defrauded. The Law of Moses said to add 20% for restitution (Leviticus 5:16). Zacchaeus goes beyond that amount. True repentance flows from a changed heart; it also shows itself in concrete actions.

Implicit in this episode is the need to have faith in Jesus Christ. What and how much did Zacchaeus know about Jesus? Early in Luke (3:8), John the Baptist told those who would come to Jesus that they must show the fruits of repentance. Isn't that what Zacchaeus was doing? Isn't he acting with faith in Jesus? Jesus said, "Today, salvation, has come to this house." If Zacchaeus was a son of Abraham, then he was a person of faith. It is wonderful that salvation came to Zacchaeus and his house; in fact, salvation was coming to all those who lived in Jericho. Even more, it is wonderful that salvation comes to your house and to my house. But do we really want Jesus to come home with us? Will we take the riches out of our lives so we can climb a tree to see Jesus?

CHAPTER 28

By What Authority?

"On one of the days while He was teaching the people in the temple and preaching the gospel, the chief priests and the scribes with the elders confronted Him, and they spoke, saying to Him, 'Tell us by what authority You are doing these things, or who is the one who gave You this authority?' Jesus answered and said to them, 'I will also ask you a question, and you tell Me: Was the baptism of John from heaven or from men?' They reasoned among themselves, saying, if we say, 'From heaven,' He will say, 'Why did you not believe him?' But if we say, 'From men, all the people will stone us to death, for they are convinced that John was a prophet.' So, they answered that they did not know where it came from. And Jesus said to them, 'Nor, will I tell you by what authority I do these things.'"
(Luke 20:1-8 NASV)

Did Jesus have the right to teach the gospel in the Temple? The Jewish guardians of the Temple, had not authorized Jesus to teach; why would He presume to enter the obvious, physical symbol of their spiritual heritage, and then hold sway over those who had come to worship? He might teach in the synagogues, but not here. Jesus' earthly ministry was mainly conducted far away from Jerusalem; now He finds a pulpit in the inner sanctum of Judaism. Were their questions and intent genuine? No. They were seeking to destroy Jesus (Luke 19:47).

By what authority is a good question. Anyone teaching false doctrine must be challenged. From the beginning, Jesus worked and taught with authority (Luke 4:1, 14, 31). Now, that authority is questioned. Jesus didn't say: You have no right to ask your questions; there was no evasion of the issue of authority. But His unexpected way of answering exposed the hypocrisy of the Jewish leaders. The Jews knew about John the Baptist; they rejected his teaching; they refused to be baptized by John (Luke 7:29-35). If John's teaching came from heaven, why would they reject him? They did reject Jesus. We are not surprised.

Consider this excerpt from *Jesus The Master Respondent*, by James D. Bales. "Some critics of the Bible have complained that Jesus did not deal fairly with His questioners...He changed the subject to John...First, he who asks a question asks a favor...He who asks a favor should be willing to do a favor...One is not automatically obligated to answer another person's questions...they (the Jews) had no right to complain...they had started the discussion with a question of their own...they were trying to trap and discredit Him (Jesus)...the answer to your own question may contain the answer to their question...He (the questioner) is more apt to see and accept the answer when he is led to answer it himself...it (Jesus' question) calls on the other person to take a position...it (Jesus' question) may stimulate the individual to think...The only way out of a genuine dilemma is to give up the error which involved one in the dilemma...Jesus' opponents realized they were in a dilemma...if they answered one way they discredited themselves...if the other way they would be forced to acknowledge the authority of Jesus."

When faced with questions that concern our relationship to Jesus, what do we do? We can evade, posture, seek inconsistencies in others, and get angry; or, we can be honest and yield to heaven's will. Now, answer Jesus' question.

CHAPTER 29

Things to Come

"Then He continued by saying to them, Nation will rise against nation and kingdom against kingdom, and there will be great earthquakes, and in various places plagues and famines; and there will be terrors and great signs from heaven. But before all these things, they will lay their hands on you and will persecute you, delivering you to the synagogues and prisons, bringing you before kings and governors for My name's sake. It will lead to an opportunity for your testimony. So, make up your minds not to prepare beforehand to defend yourselves; for I will give you utterance and wisdom which none of your opponents will be able to resist or refute. But you will be betrayed even by parents and brothers and relatives and friends, and they will put some of you to death, and you will be hated by all because of My name. Yet not a hair of your head will perish. By your endurance you will gain your lives."
(Luke 21:10-19 NASV)

In 586 BC the Babylonians destroyed the temple King Solomon had built years earlier (970 BC). Even though the Jews who returned from captivity rebuilt the temple, an older generation lamented the lost glory and beauty of the original. "Who is left among you who saw this temple in its former glory? And how do you see it now? Does it not seem to you like nothing in comparison?" (Haggai 2:3). John 2:20 refers to King Herod's temple renovation, a project that actually extended beyond his lifetime. The temple was in the heart of Jerusalem—city center. More, the temple was the heart and life of Judaism. The temple was where Israel met with God. Early in life, Jesus made two trips to Jerusalem. Now, the temple would be destroyed. Why? There were clues; yet, the money changers, religious leaders, and hard-hearted Jews missed the true significance of the temple; it was time for a cleansing. The life and death and teaching of Jesus, the one who is greater than the temple, said it was time for judgment to come on the recalcitrant Jewish nation. The chosen people of God, with all of the hopes and dreams and possibilities imaginable, rejected not only the prophets of God, but also, the greatest prophet of all. They soon cried: Crucify Him! Crucify Him!

Using Old Testament judgment language, Jesus said nations would turn on each other. Natural disasters would occur (Ezekiel 36:29-30). Prepare to stand strong; you will be persecuted in the synagogues. In Acts, Luke tells that story repeatedly, especially early in the life of the church. This would be the time to give up; instead, this was an opportunity to show their faith in Christ, their testimony. The apostles were able to preach faithfully even as they were thrown into prison. Jesus said: don't be so concerned about these matters that you deliberate constantly about how to persevere. Even your loved ones will turn against you. Chaos ensued when the Roman army surrounded the city and destroyed the temple. A cause for concern? Yes! Still, Jesus said: Not a hair of your head will perish. Did some Christians die during these times? But even if they died, were they really dead? No. They were alive in Christ. The disciples asked questions about the temple and the city. Jesus said times will be tough but you will live. When the Roman armies come to our city, into our lives, when our struggles increase, what can we do? Jesus said: Endure and then you will live.

CHAPTER 30

The Lord's Supper

"When the hour had come, He reclined at the table, and the apostles with Him. And He said to them, I have earnestly desired to eat this Passover with you before I suffer; for I say to you, I shall never again eat it until it is fulfilled in the kingdom of God. And when He had taken a cup and given thanks, He said, take this and share it among yourselves; for I say to you, I will not drink of the fruit of the vine from now on until the kingdom of God comes. And when He had taken some bread and given thanks, He broke it and gave it to them, saying, this is My body which is given for you; do this in remembrance of Me. And in the same way He took the cup after they had eaten, saying, this cup which is poured out for you is the new covenant in My blood. But behold, the hand of the one betraying Me is with Mine on the table. For indeed, the Son of Man is going as it has been determined; but woe to that man by whom He is betrayed! And they began to discuss among themselves which one of them it might be who was going to do this thing."
(Luke 22:14-23 NASV)

The ability to remember can be a blessing. We can recall, reflect on, and dwell on the past. When our memories are good and pleasant, we appreciate that ability. If our memories are not pleasant, we can still learn from the past, make amends, and go forward. We need to remember that we are God's children; our spiritual identity should ever be on our hearts and then faithfully displayed each day. We have tombstones to remember the dead; we have monuments to remind us about some who were integral to the founding and maintaining of our nation. The Sabbath was a memorial for God's people. Annual feasts—the Passover, First Fruits, Pentecost—reminded the Jews that they owed their very lives, physically and spiritually, to Jehovah.

In partaking of the Last Supper with His disciples, Jesus said: This do in remembrance of Me. This memorial, a part of Luke's narrative, explained who Jesus was. The Lord's Supper helps us know the identity of Christ; it helps us remember who we are supposed to be. In partaking of the cup, representing the shed blood of Christ, we are communing with our Savior. We are participating in an act of worship that helps us recall the death of Christ. "Is not the cup of blessing which we bless a sharing in the blood of Christ? Is not the bread which we break a sharing in the body of Christ?" (1 Corinthians 10:16-17). Christ's blood redeems us from sin. "Knowing that you were not redeemed with perishable things like silver or gold from your futile way of life inherited from your forefathers, but with precious blood, as of a lamb unblemished and spotless, the blood of Christ" (1 Peter 1:18-19). "Much more then, having now been justified by His blood" (Romans 5:9). Now, followers of Christ are His body; we are the church of Christ. Jesus "tasted death for every man" (Hebrews 2:9). His body was nailed to a Roman cross. We are His spiritual body. "And He put all things in subjection under His feet, and gave Him as head over all things to the church, which is His body, the fullness of Him who fills all in all" (Ephesians 1:22-23). We worship on the Lord's Day, the day when His church was established, the day He was raised from the grave. On that day we remember the Lord's death (Acts 20:7). Who would disagree about the need to consistently, faithfully, fervently, commune with Christ and with His people? Let us sing: "Lead Me to Calvary…Lest we forget."

CHAPTER 31

Simon of Cyrene

"When they led Him away, they seized a man, Simon of Cyrene, coming in from the country, and placed on him the cross to carry behind Jesus."
(Luke 23:26 NASV)

Jesus often said that He would take up His cross. His time had arrived. The Sanhedrin, led by Annas and Caiaphas, condemned Him. Pilate washed his hands of the matter. Jesus, a condemned man, walks to His death, carrying His own cross. The crowds clamored for His death. Some were laughing; some were crying. The Father was watching. Thousands of Roman crosses had cast their blighted shadows upon the empire. Now, in a back-water part of the world, one cross would stand higher and shine brighter than any before.

Condemned men were forced to carry the crossbeam; it was then fixed to an upright timber already in ground. The man to be executed might wear a sign of some kind around his neck, a declaration of guilt. That sign would be attached to the top of the cross. Ropes were sometimes used to tie the condemned to the cross; in Jesus' case, nails were used. Life could linger for several days before death finally came from exposure, asphyxia, or loss of blood. Can we imagine the pain Jesus experienced after being scourged? The cross was now too heavy for Jesus to carry. Roman citizens were too good to carry this instrument of shame. What to do?

Simon of Cyrene (north Africa) is conscripted (laid hold of), becoming part of that eventful day. Many speculate (with good cause?) that because Simon and his two sons are mentioned by name (*a* Rufus is mentioned in

Romans 16:13), that he was well known to some in the New Testament, and possibly Mark knew him personally. Simon, a common Jewish name, was in Jerusalem for the Passover. Now, he would carry his own cross; and he would carry Jesus' cross. Was Simon glad to identify with Jesus and to carry the shame and alienation of the cross? Or, was he simply there on that day along with many others watching as the horrors of crucifixion were carried out?

The call to discipleship involves a cross, Jesus' cross and our own. Luke speaks of this often. For three years Jesus had invited all who would come to follow Him to take up their crosses, and walk the road to pain, humility, and death. Death to self, to sin, to anything that prevents the advent of kingdom into one's heart are the demands of the cross. Do we see in Simon someone who is now following Jesus, who seeks true holiness, and now wants to serve others, even to the point of death? Or, do we see too much?

Could Simon ever dream that he would play such a role on that great day; or, that now 2,000 years later, we would be talking about him? We don't know much about Simon; the same can be said about most of us. We live and toil in a big, wide world. Most people don't know us, or even care to know. That's ok. We must remember that Jesus died on a cross to give us life. And He died for Simon. Have you ever wondered if Simon talked to his boys, Alexander and Rufus, about what happened that day? Have we talked to our children about what happened that day?

CHAPTER 32

He Has Risen

"He is not here, but He has risen. Remember how He spoke to you while He was still in Galilee, saying that the Son of Man must be delivered into the hands of sinful men, and be crucified, and the third day rise again. And they remembered His words."
(Luke 24:6-8 NASV)

Luke used words to tell the story of Jesus. The Apostles preached words of salvation: words given by the Holy Spirit. Jesus' words are important. Now, after the horrors of the cross, we have the words of Jesus Himself. Jesus said that He would die and then be raised. Why be surprised that the tomb was empty? After all, Jesus' words are always true; He said He would be raised. Who remembered His words? Initially the women came to the tomb to anoint the body of Jesus; they expected to find Him in the tomb. But they finally remembered His words about His resurrection. Not surprisingly, it was Mary the mother of James, Mary Magdalene, Joanna, and other unnamed women who remembered what Jesus had previously said. These women reported the empty tomb to the apostles. Yet, the men who had been with Jesus for three years, the men who had heard the same words as the women, refused to accept their eyewitness testimony. "Now they were Mary Magdalene and Joanna and Mary the mother of James; also, the other women with them were telling these things to the apostles. But these words appeared to them as nonsense, and they would not believe them" (Luke 24:10-11). Were these women hysterical? Were they uttering nonsense? Strong biases against the testimony of women existed in the first century. Peter, though, got up and ran to the tomb; he left in wonder about what had happened. Was he thinking about Jesus' words? Only a few days before, after Peter denied the Lord and remembered the words of Jesus, "how He had told him, before a rooster crows today, you will deny me three times" (Luke 22:61).

What was Peter remembering now? After Jesus' death by crucifixion, could it be possible that He was alive? Was reality sinking in? What about these women? They were not simply "eleventh hour" disciples. They had been with Jesus from the beginning (Luke 8:1-3). Jesus had restored human life (Luke 7:10-17; John 11). Jesus had actually died; the Romans knew what they were doing when they nailed someone to a cross. How can Joseph of Arimathea, who is in all four gospels, be discounted? Too many people knew him to believe that he was a figment of the gospel writers' imagination? All four gospels mention the discovery of the empty tomb by the women. If you were trying to manufacture some elaborate tale about Jesus, you wouldn't use the testimony of women. What about the many witnesses to the resurrection? Paul spoke about many of these people still being alive at the time he wrote to the Corinthians (1 Corinthians 15:1-11). It would take lots of work to discredit 500 witnesses.

Finally, the transformed lives of the New Testament Christians we read about in Acts, Revelation, and throughout the New Testament, say something about the power and reality of the resurrection. Jesus always joined His actions and deeds with words of explanation. Those words need to be remembered. When your life is in shambles, or when you have a crisis of faith, remember these words: He is not here; He has risen!

CHAPTER 33

You Shall Be My Witnesses

"The former account I made, O Theophilus, of all that Jesus began both to do and teach, until the day in which He was taken up, after He through the Holy Spirit had given commandments to the apostles whom He had chosen, to whom He also presented Himself alive after His suffering by many infallible proofs, being seen by them during forty days and speaking of the things pertaining to the kingdom of God."
(Acts 1:1-3)

Upon reading these opening words of Acts, the natural question to ask is: What is the "former account" Luke refers to? We generally understand that this refers to the Gospel of Luke; we also understand that Luke was the writer of both books. We also understand that the Gospel of Luke tells us about Jesus; Acts tells us about His people, the church. Volumes have been written about such matters; you could easily become a "specialist" in technical matters relating to both books.

Acts is an interesting book. It is filled with action, persecution, preaching, deceit, jailbreaks, shipwrecks, and pathos. Judaism sometimes and Christianity often, take center stage. Acts provokes lots of discussion about the church, the apostles, and the Holy Spirit. It has been used as a guide for fulfilling the Great Commission of Christ. Luke introduces us to interesting people—Saul of Tarsus, Peter, Philip, and a myriad of antagonists. How can New Testament Christians *not* be drawn to the *"Hub of the Bible?"* (book by James D. Bales). The spokes on the wagon wheel jut out in all directions, taking us to very real people—people who knew and followed Jesus Christ, the very one of whom Luke wrote. Acts, like the Gospel of Luke, is addressed to the "most excellent" Theophilus (Luke 1:3). Was he a highly placed Roman official? Was he the prototype of all who had an interest in hearing about Jesus? His name means "friend" or "lover of God." Whoever he was, Luke dedicates his book to him; such dedications were common in the first century. It is good that Luke tells the story of Jesus' followers. These followers coalesced around their risen Savior, anticipating the advent of the kingdom. The decision to follow Jesus would bring salvation; it would also bring persecution, a theme running through Acts. In a very real way, the book of Acts answers the question: Will the followers of the risen Christ continue in their faith and service to Him? There is evidence of success in their efforts. The unfolding of their story is what Luke writes about.

"But you shall receive power when the Holy Spirit has come upon you; and you shall be witnesses to Me in Jerusalem, and in all Judea and Samaria, and to the end of the earth" (Acts 1:8). Specifically, the Apostles of Christ were His witnesses; they were eyewitnesses of Jesus' resurrection. We see the risen Christ by the eye of faith. Still, though, we carry forth that same message as citizens in His kingdom. We carry forth that message, sometimes in the midst of persecution. We carry forth that message, buoyed by the early faith and success of our spiritual ancestors. If this is not true for you, then get busy reading Luke's letter to Theophilus.

CHAPTER 34

The Resurrection of Christ

"The former account I made, O Theophilus, of all that Jesus began both to do and teach, until the day in which He was taken up, after He through the Holy Spirit had given commandments to the apostles whom He had chosen, to whom He also presented Himself alive after His suffering by many infallible proofs, being seen by them during forty days and speaking of the things pertaining to the kingdom of God."
(Acts 1:1-3)

The Bible is not exhaustive (John 20:30-31; Acts 20:35). That is, it does not contain everything Christ did or said; it does not contain myriads of details you and I wonder about. The Bible often summarizes the activities of God's out-working of His eternal purpose. It gives us snapshots of what Jesus was doing and saying. This opening passage from Luke tells us that for a period of forty days Jesus spoke about the kingdom of God. What does that mean? Who did Jesus talk to? Where did He go? We can know some things about this period of time; yet, many questions can be raised that have no direct answers.

Luke sets the stage for the main message of Apostolic preaching—namely, the resurrection of Jesus Christ. "During" or "over" a period of forty days, Jesus demonstrated to many eye-witnesses that He was alive. Jesus spoke to two men on the Emmaus Road (Luke 24:13-27). Paul emphasized this same message in 1 Corinthians 15. "He was buried, and that He rose again the third day according to the Scriptures, and that He was seen by Cephas, then by the twelve. After that He was seen by over five hundred brethren at once, of whom the greater part remain to the present, but some have fallen asleep. After that He was seen by James, then by all the apostles. Then last of all He was seen by me also, as by one born out of due time" (15:4-8).

Christ's resurrection was the prelude to the Gospel of the Kingdom. God is sovereign; He reigns over His creation. Psalm 103:19 says, "The LORD has established His throne in heaven, and His kingdom rules over all." He reigned over Israel; now, He seeks kingdom citizens who will accept the authority of His Son. Those who will allow Christ to reign in their lives become His people, kingdom citizens, the church. In Acts, Jesus is the obvious subject of kingdom preaching. In Samaria when Philip preached "the things concerning the kingdom of God and the name of Jesus Christ, both men and women were baptized" (Acts 8:12). Paul was "preaching the kingdom of God" (Acts 20:25). For forty days, Jesus by virtue of His resurrection validated His claim to be the Messiah, the Christ of God. He presented Himself as the fulfillment of Old Testament prophecy— prophecy that pointed to the Messianic kingdom—a kingdom over which He would be king. It then became the responsibility of the disciples to go forth into the entire world and proclaim the message of the resurrected Savior.

Jesus is in heaven. We are on earth. He gave His apostles the Great Commission; they, then, took the gospel into the entire world (Colossians 1:23). While we are 2000 years removed from that time, let us make sure that we don't turn Christ's Great Commission into the Great Omission.

CHAPTER 35

The Holy Spirit

"When the Day of Pentecost had fully come, they were all with one accord in one place. And suddenly there came a sound from heaven, as of a rushing mighty wind, and it filled the whole house where they were sitting. Then there appeared to them divided tongues, as of fire, and one sat upon each of them. And they were all filled with the Holy Spirit and began to speak with other tongues, as the Spirit gave them utterance."
(Acts 2:1-4)

The expansion of the gospel in the first century was inextricably tied to the Holy Spirit of God. While the Old Testament doesn't develop a *systematic theology* of the Holy Spirit (that is, the Old Testament says some things about the Spirit, but not very much), the New Testament does. John the Baptist in warning the unrepentant Jews, said that Jesus would "baptize" them in judgment and in the Holy Spirit (Matthew 3:11). How would that judgment come? That is the story Luke tells, as he unfolds the early history of first century Christians. *Generally*, all people who would come to Christ would benefit from the work of the Holy Spirit of God. "All nations" (Jew and Gentile) could come to Zion, hear the message of the risen Savior, and become part of a peaceful kingdom (Isaiah 2:1-4). *Specifically*, the Apostles, as the chosen ambassadors of Christ, would be enabled by the Holy Spirit to do what Jesus told them to do in Acts 1:8. "But you shall receive power when the Holy Spirit has come upon you; and you shall be witnesses to Me in Jerusalem, and in all Judea and Samaria, and to the end of the earth." As Luke unpacks the activities of the early Christians, including the Apostles, it is clear that the gospel goes forth under the aegis of the Spirit. It is a mistake to read the words of John the Baptist in Matthew 3 and conclude that all people, everywhere, of all time, by coming to Christ, would be able under the power of the Spirit to exercise spiritual gifts. The Apostles, though, received promises from the Lord, that they, in their work, would be endowed by the Holy Spirit, which enabled them to reveal and confirm the word of Christ. John 14, 15, 16 are crucial in understanding what Jesus promised and what the Apostles would do. "However, when He, the Spirit of truth, has come, He will guide you into all truth; for He will not speak on His own authority, but whatever He hears He will speak; and He will tell you things to come" (John 16:13). The Apostles were the only men who received this promise from Christ. They were to go into the entire world, preaching the gospel, and confirm that message by signs, wonders, and miracles (Mark 16:17-20). Yes, spiritual gifts were exercised in the early church; each gift was appropriated according to the rationale of the Lord (1 Corinthians 12:18). Some early Christians had gifts (1 Corinthians 12); some did not (Acts 8). The promises in the gospel of John to the Apostles are specific to these chosen agents of Christ.

Acts 2 opens with the fulfillment of the prophecy from Joel (Joel 2:28-32), the words of John the Baptist (Matthew 3:11), and the words of Jesus (John 14, 15, 16). "Fullness" runs throughout the book of Acts. It was the "fullness of time" (Galatians 4:4). And the Apostles were "filled" with the Holy Spirit. In languages known by the people gathered in Jerusalem, the gospel went forth into some good and honest hearts. Eventually, that gospel went into the entire world (Colossians 1:23). We have that gospel today. Today, we continue to be blessed by the Holy Spirit of God.

CHAPTER 36

Repent and Be Baptized

"Then Peter said to them, 'Repent, and let every one of you be baptized in the name of Jesus Christ for the remission of sins; and you shall receive the gift of the Holy Spirit.'"
(Acts 2:38)

Faithful preachers should be concerned about being effective in their preaching of God's word. Most are. Preachers rejoice when people are "cut to the heart." A conscience that is alive to the Lord and His will can be anxious or remorseful about its actions. This kind of conscience shows humility—the hearer knows her need for repentance—change—and knows that a needed message has been preached—hope. All of these elements are involved in the first gospel sermon preached in the name of the risen Savior as recorded in Acts 2.

Those guilty of crucifying the Son of God were anguished at their actions. They needed to repent. Repentance involves a complete change of heart and then the confession of sin. True repentance is the by-product of "godly sorrow" (2 Corinthians 7:10). This was the message of John the Baptist and Jesus; it is now the message of the Apostles, who preached under the authority of Christ. Luke 24:47 says "that repentance and remission of sins should be preached in His name to all nations, beginning at Jerusalem."

Peter's admonition in Acts 2:38 was spoken to those gathered in Jerusalem. No longer would the Jews think in "corporate" terms; that is, national concepts or fleshly family connections would give way to a personal decision to yield to Christ. The "new covenant" was for all from the "least of them to the greatest of them" (Hebrews 8:11). Peter says that repentance and baptism was to be done "in the name of Jesus Christ." This is common to preaching in the book of Acts (Acts 10:48; Acts 8:16; Acts 19:5). When obeying the gospel, one would be "calling on the name of the Lord." This was anticipated by Old Testament prophets (Joel 2:28-32); Peter appropriates this "call" in his sermon.

Peter says that those who repented and were baptized would receive "the gift of the Holy Spirit." Scholars of the Greek language tell us that "the gift of the Holy Spirit" can be the Holy Spirit Himself; or, the gift can be what the Holy Spirit gives. Yes, the Apostles received the Holy Spirit on the Day of Pentecost; they were able to preach their sermon in languages known to the people in Jerusalem. Yes, as the church grew and the gospel was spread from Jerusalem and then to "Judea and Samaria, and to the end of the earth" (Acts 1:8), spiritual gifts were given for the maturation of the early church. And yes, the Bible says that the Holy Spirit dwells in the child of God (2 Corinthians 1:22). There are "gifts of the Spirit" and there is the "fruit of the Spirit."

Acts 2:39 helps us understand what Acts 2:38 means. "For the promise is to you and to your children, and to all who are afar off, as many as the Lord our God will call." The promise made to Abraham in Genesis 12:1-3 finds ultimate fulfillment in the advent, life, death, and resurrection of Jesus Christ. The salvation He provides is His gift to us. The message Peter and others were preaching was done under the aegis of the Spirit. The gift of the Holy Spirit is the message of salvation—salvation that is found only in Jesus. No wonder the people were pricked in their hearts. The question is: Are we?

CHAPTER 37

Added to the Church

> "So continuing daily with one accord in the temple, and breaking bread from house to house, they ate their food with gladness and simplicity of heart, praising God and having favor with all the people. And the Lord added to the church daily those who were being saved."
> (Acts 2:46-47)

This passage reveals that these early disciples (they were not called Christians until Acts 11:26!) began in earnest to acclimate themselves to the will of their Savior. They continued to engage in doing Christ's will. They were happy to be a part of the Lord's church. They were living out their faith every day. They associated together. And in some general way, they found a measure of good will from the citizens in Jerusalem. They were serving the Lord *everyday*! As Jews, they still had an affinity for the temple; the house of God provided a convenient gathering place for these 3,000 children of God.

Soon, though, others were added to the number of believers. The people who were added to the church were those who did as the 3,000 had done—that is, they heard the word of God, repented of their sins, and were baptized into Christ; He added them to His church. Jesus promised to build His church (Matthew 16:18). The church, or *ekklesia*, the called-out body, is people—people who have yielded their hearts to Christ. The church is people who are in covenant relationship with Christ. The church is people who have heard and obeyed the gospel; the church is people who continue to hear and obey the gospel. Simplicity or singleness of heart characterized these early saints. Their hearts were centered on one thing, and one thing only—Jesus! That kind of commitment not only set a good example; it undoubtedly, caused others to consider who Jesus was, resulting in their obedience. The old King James version of Acts 2:47 says, "Praising God, and having favour with all the people. And the Lord added to the church daily such as should be saved." "Such as should be saved" are those who should be saved! That is, these people are the ones, the only ones, who came to Christ to be washed clean in His blood. The church is people—people who are saved from sin.

If you, in obedient faith (with all that this entails), come to Christ, the only place you can be is in His church. This is not an institution. This is not a building. This is not a social or recreational gathering. It is a spiritual relationship with Christ. The church belongs to Him. He has the right to tell us what we must do in order to be saved. He adds us to His saved body. Salvation is in Christ; salvation is not in the church. The church saves no one. Jesus is the world's only Savior. The saved are the church. The church is people. It was that way 2,000 years ago. It is the same today.

CHAPTER 38

Silver and Gold

"Then Peter said, 'Silver and gold I do not have, but what I do have I give you: In the name of Jesus Christ of Nazareth, rise up and walk.'"
(Acts 3:6)

The fact that Peter and John went to the temple to pray shows that these early Christians, still Jews by birth, did not immediately throw off all the vestiges of Judaism. In one sense, they were doing what Jesus told them to do—they were "beginning in Jerusalem" with the message of salvation; soon, the 3,000 were supplemented with others; the church grew, eventually being hounded out of Jerusalem by persecution. Still, though, the apostles, early on, used the city as their base of operations. It was the "ninth" hour, or, 3 p.m., our time.

Acts 3:2 says, "And a certain man lame from his mother's womb was carried, whom they laid daily at the gate of the temple which is called Beautiful, to ask alms from those who entered the temple." The exact location of the gate called Beautiful is not clear. McGarvey said: "The beautiful gate of the temple, so called because of its magnificent folding doors, fifty feet high and forty feet wide, covered with gold...was the favorite pass-way into the temple" (Commentary, *Acts*, 51). From this vantage point, with people coming and going at all hours, the beggar had many opportunities to try to get some help.

Rather than giving the beggar alms, Peter said, "I will give you something more valuable than silver and gold." Peter gave him the greatest gift possible. Peter gave him the opportunity to know who Jesus was. Yes, a miracle was worked. Yes, the man could get up and walk, leap, and praise God. But there was more; there was the message of salvation. As on Pentecost, Peter pointed to the guilt of the people who gathered to listen. "The God of Abraham, Isaac, and Jacob, the God of our fathers, glorified His Servant Jesus, whom you delivered up and denied in the presence of Pilate, when he was determined to let Him go" (Acts 3:13).

"Repent therefore and be converted, that your sins may be blotted out, so that times of refreshing may come from the presence of the Lord" (Acts 3:19). Inherent in Peter's message is the need for faith. Faith comes by hearing God's word (Romans 10:17). But true, saving faith, involves repentance. The basic theme of Peter's second sermon in Acts 3 is the same as Acts 2—namely, the people directly addressed were guilty of rejecting and crucifying the Son of God. They needed to repent of their sins. While repentance involves turning from sin (that is, you need to stop doing what is wrong), it also involves godly sorrow (2 Corinthians 7:10). You can have godly sorrow that leads to life; this kind of sorrow brings no regret because you are turning away from sin. Or, you can have worldly sorrow; this kind of sorrow brings further pain and spiritual destruction because you are not really repenting of your sins. The people in Jerusalem needed to "turn" from their sins. Sorrow for sin can lead you to stop doing what is wrong; but it takes godly sorrow to produce true repentance; the result is true conversion to the Lord.

What is the point? The point is this: If you are lost in sin, alienated from the Lord, heading for hell, would you rather have silver and gold, or, the message of Jesus that tells you of His love and death and salvation. Who knows what you might receive the next time you sit down at the gate of the temple!

CHAPTER 39

Opposition to the Gospel

> "Now as they spoke to the people, the priests, the captain of the temple, and the Sadducees came upon them, being greatly disturbed that they taught the people and preached in Jesus the resurrection from the dead. And they laid hands on them, and put them in custody until the next day, for it was already evening. However, many of those who heard the word believed; and the number of the men came to be about five thousand."
> (Acts 4:1-3)

The time and place in which we live produces some, but not much, opposition to the gospel. Yes, "religious freedoms" are being chipped away by those who have turned from God. Sadly, this erosion of basic principles of honesty, ethical behavior, and even a basic commitment to some kind of "higher being" often comes from our nation's leaders. Too, the liberal media engages constantly in a barrage of insults against people of faith. Still, though, there are lots of places in our world where "Christian faith" of most any kind is rejected and often, openly persecuted. It is clear from the early years of the Lord's church in the first century that this was true, too. Peter and John were having great success in preaching the message of Jesus. With that success, strong opposition came from the ruling Jewish leaders in Jerusalem.

"And it came to pass, on the next day, that their rulers, elders, and scribes, as well as Annas the high priest, Caiaphas, John, and Alexander, and as many as were of the family of the high priest, were gathered together at Jerusalem" (Acts 4:5-6). Annas was High Priest from AD 6-15; his son-in-law Caiaphas was high priest AD 18-37. Annas was high priest "emeritus." The high priestly family controlled the temple; in controlling the temple, they controlled the money—they were rich men! Jesus often condemned the hypocrisy of the Pharisees (Matthew 23). Apostolic preaching of the resurrection would naturally arouse suspicion from the Sadducees, who did not believe in the resurrection (Acts 23:8). More, though, the success of the gospel meant that many would turn away from the temple and the leaders were afraid of losing control. Their reaction was not new. Mark 15:10 says: "For he knew that the chief priests had delivered him for envy." Remember, Annas and his family were involved in the trials and subsequent death of Jesus (John 18:13-14). Jesus who claimed to be greater than the temple was rejected. Now, the message of His resurrection was rejected. Now Peter and John were hauled before these authorities.

"And when they had set them in the midst, they asked, 'By what power or by what name have you done this?'" (Acts 4:7). The Apostles were called to account for their actions. Who gave them authority to heal the lame man? That man was there, too (Acts 4:14); they could not deny that he could now walk. Now, though, what thoughts, what memories washed over the minds of these two men? Would they recall that only a few days prior their Savior faced similar accusations? Would they remember Jesus' resolute determination to be "faithful unto death"? Would they remember that in that moment of crisis, they had turned and fled (Matthew 26:56)? Whether in times of persecution or times of relative peace remember that the resurrected Jesus calls us to stand before the world, before our loved ones, before our own conscience, and answer the question: Who gave you authority to live the way you live?

CHAPTER 40

Barnabas

"And Joseph, who by the apostles was surnamed Barnabas (which is, being interpreted, Son of exhortation), a Levite, a man of Cyprus by race, having a field, sold it, and brought the money and laid it at the apostles' feet."
(Acts 4:36-37 ASV)

Barnabas is one of the bright spots in the early church. Luke tells us that Barnabas' name (in Hebrew) means "Son of exhortation." Joseph, his Jewish name, was used at home and in the synagogue; Barnabas was his descriptive name. His name in the Greek language is *paraklesis*.

The *Blue Letter Bible* gives this definition of *paraklesis*: "a calling near, summons, (esp. for help), importation, supplication, entreaty, exhortation, admonition, encouragement, consolation, comfort, solace; that which affords comfort or refreshment." This is closely akin to the promise Jesus made to His apostles in John 14:16. "And I will pray the Father, and he shall give you another Comforter, that he may be with you forever." Barnabas is featured often in the book of Acts. He traveled with Paul. He was a cousin to John Mark (Colossians 4:10).

Barnabas was an encouragement to people. How so? From reading the last part of Acts 4, we learn that these early disciples banded together, drawn to each other by persecution. Many of them were yet away from home, having come to Jerusalem for Pentecost; evidently many of them stayed. Being away from home they did not have access to their own private belongings; staying in Jerusalem created lots of needs for lots of people. Their needs were willingly met by others. Acts 4:34 says, "For neither was there among them any that lacked: for as many as were possessors of lands or houses sold them, and brought the prices of the things that were sold." Barnabas participated in the funding of these needs. The Holy Spirit didn't simply say: Barnabas was a generous man. The Holy Spirit told us what Barnabas did in being generous. Why was he singled out for notice by Luke? Is it because he is so often, later in the book of Acts, featured prominently in preaching and traveling activities for the Lord?

What Barnabas did was an unselfish act of love. He along with other believers "were of one heart and soul" (Acts 4:32). Even though the field belonged to him (Acts 5:4), he was willing to take his proceeds and give it to others who had needs. Paul, citing the example of Christ, says, "In all things I gave you an example, that so laboring ye ought to help the weak, and to remember the words of the Lord Jesus, that he himself said, It is more blessed to give than to receive" (Acts 20:35). Paul lived that way; so did Barnabas. And so do many Christians today. Today, there are many Christians, by their sacrifice and generosity to others, give great encouragement—encouragement to those who may be "down and out," to those who are struggling, to those who need some help "getting back on their feet." These folks are not stingy. They are generous. So was Barnabas.

How we spend our money says something about our love for God. Fellowship, the Bible, prayer, worship—all of these spiritual concerns and more, are important. We can pretend to pray. We can pretend to worship. We can pretend to study our Bibles. But we can't pretend to give up what we have for the blessing and benefit of others. Our use of our money shows us up for who we really are. The apostles changed Joseph's name to Barnabas because that's who he was. Now his name matched his life. Who are you? What is your name?

CHAPTER 41

Ananias and Sapphira

"But a certain man named Ananias, with Sapphira his wife, sold a possession, and kept back part of the price, his wife also being privy to it, and brought a certain part, and laid it at the apostles' feet. Peter said, Ananias, why hath Satan filled thy heart to lie to the Holy Spirit, and to keep back part of the price of the land? While it remained, did it not remain thine own? and after it was sold, was it not in thy power? How is it that thou hast conceived this thing in thy heart? Thou has not lied unto men, but unto God. And Ananias hearing these words fell down and gave up the ghost...three hours after, when his wife, not knowing what was done, came in. Peter answered...Tell me whether ye sold the land for so much. And she said, Yea, for so much...Peter said to her, How is it that ye have agreed together to try the Spirit of the Lord? Behold, the feet of them that have buried thy husband are at the door, and they shall carry thee out...she fell down immediately...and gave up the ghost... and great fear came upon the whole church."
(Acts 5:1-11)

Make no mistake about it: Satan will do anything he can do to hinder the spread of the gospel. The early success of God's people in the first century inspires and encourages present-day believers. But let us also be reminded that the devil will use any means available to disrupt any progress God's people might be making. In this case, he worked through the greed of two Christians, Ananias and Sapphira, to cause trouble for the Lord's church.

Comparisons between this couple and Barnabas are inevitable. They did the same thing; they both sold a piece of property. They both brought the proceeds to the apostles to be used appropriately. Barnabas brought all the money generated by his transaction; Ananias and Sapphira contributed only a part of the money. Was there something wrong with them doing this? Peter indicates that the property was their own; and the proceeds belonged to them after the sale. What was the problem? Did they intend to give all but didn't do so? They weren't necessarily obligated to give all; but the fact that Peter rebuked Ananias initially indicates a problem. Then Sapphira lied about the entire matter. Their honesty is questionable. And more, their integrity must be called into question. They brought only a part but pretended to bring the whole.

It is a serious matter to present ourselves as faithful children of God when the reality of our lives says otherwise. We might, as did the Pharisee of Luke 18, talk of all we do to serve the Lord—we go to church, we pray, we read the Bible, we even give of our means—when down deep, we know the truth about our profession of faith. We know, if we will answer rightly to the conscience, that there is a gap between what we say we are and what we really are. Engaging in exercises of spiritual self-deception is dangerous. It is dangerous to lie to ourselves. It is dangerous to lie to God. If the devil cannot destroy the Lord's church from without, he will try to destroy it from within. Hypocrisy, rebellion, and stubbornness are his tools. Our use of money is one of our greatest challenges. Don't play into Satan's hands.

CHAPTER 42

We Must Obey God

Often, the apostles faced the open antagonism of the Sadducees. The first mention of this Jewish sect is dated from the time of John Hyrcanus, 135-104BC (Hyrcanus was part of the Hasmonean Dynasty; he led resistance efforts against the Egyptians; siding first with the Pharisees, he soon switched allegiance to the Sadducees; consequently, along with the Sadducees, he was able to control the temple and thus controlled the money; that control was still viable in New Testament times). "Then the high priest rose up, and all those who were with him (which is the sect of the Sadducees), and they were filled with indignation, and laid their hands on the apostles and put them in the common prison" (Acts 5:17-18). Charged not to speak in Christ's name, Peter replied: "We must obey God rather than men" (Acts 5:29 ASV).

Imprisonment for these preachers in the New Testament was common. Peter (Acts 12), Paul and Silas (Acts 16), and Paul (Acts 25-28), were imprisoned. In Acts 5 an angel unlocked the door; in Acts 12 an angel unlocked the door; in Acts 16 an earthquake secured the release of the prisoners. It wasn't true, though, that every preacher in prison was released this way. Evidently, Paul was in prison at the end of his life; it is clear that he was expecting death (2 Timothy 4:6-8). This time, in Acts 5, it was "the angel of the Lord" who brought the apostles out of prison. While *angel* can mean simply *messenger*, here it seems that God Himself was directly involved in securing the release of His servants. This would be the same "angel of the Lord" mentioned in Acts 7:30—here, it is none other than the Great "I AM" mentioned in Exodus 3. The Lord told the apostles to continue to preach "to the people all the words of this life" (Acts 5:20).

Regardless of these troubled times for these early Christians, they continued to be faithful in doing what the Lord had told them to do, namely, they began in "Jerusalem" and then went to "Judea and Samaria" and finally to "the end of the earth" (Acts 1:8). Colossians 1:23 says something about the spread of the gospel in the first century. "If indeed you continue in the faith, grounded and steadfast, and are not moved away from the hope of the gospel which you heard, which was preached to every creature under heaven, of which I, Paul, became a minister." Without arguing about whether Babylon was Rome or some other place (1 Peter 5:13), Peter indicates that his life was spent preaching the gospel (2 Peter 1:19-21). John was still "plugging away" when the New Testament comes to an end (Revelation 1:10). And whether Paul ever made it to Spain or not, it is still clear that he continued his work as the minister to the Gentiles (Acts 9:15; Romans 15:24).

What is the point? The point is, that when we are absolutely convinced, when we absolutely believe with all of our hearts that we should obey God rather than men, we, too, will be active and persistent in spreading the gospel. It won't matter about persecution; it won't matter about our own desires; it won't matter about the Pharisees or Sadducees; it won't matter about most everything else. While Peter and John were disobeying the civil authorities in Jerusalem, they were justified by a higher authority— the authority of God. When we get that right, we will always obey God rather than men.

CHAPTER 43

Serving Tables

"Now in those days, when the number of the disciples was multiplying, there arose a complaint against the Hebrews by the Hellenists, because their widows were neglected in the daily distribution. Then the twelve summoned the multitude of the disciples and said, "It is not desirable that we should leave the word of God and serve tables." Therefore, brethren, seek out from among you seven men of good reputation, full of the Holy Spirit and wisdom, whom we may appoint over this business; "but we will give ourselves continually to prayer and to the ministry of the word."
(Acts 6:1-4)

Growing pains for churches are inevitable. The unity of the church in Jerusalem hit a snag. The generosity of these early Christians made it possible for those in need of even daily, basic necessities (food), to receive what was needed to sustain them. Remember that the church in Jerusalem was still "housing" folks from lots of other places (Acts 2:9-11). Now, the Grecian widows, that is, Jews who were of foreign birth but had adopted the Greek way of life, were being neglected when the distribution of food took place. There is no hint that this neglect was deliberate. Still, the problem demanded attention. How would the problem be solved?

While taking care of such needs would have been perfectly alright even for the apostles, these chosen ambassadors of Christ recognized that they did have other work to do. Their focus was prayer and God's word. Calling all together, the "group" was told to choose among themselves, seven qualified men, to take charge of this work. Were these seven the first "deacons" in the church? Many think so, arguing from the word deacon/servant/minister. Whether yes or no, can we learn from what happened in this incident?

Spiritual service can include lots of different things. The apostles clearly had great responsibilities in preaching God's word. While we do not have living apostles today, we do have the result of their work: the word of God (Ephesians 2:20). Today, not all Christians are going to be preachers and Bible class teachers, functioning publicly in a congregation. Still, all Christians must have an interest in God's word and in prayer, even as the apostles did. The seven men who took hold of this new found work were also serving God; they were simply doing other work that needed doing. Interestingly, the men chosen all had Greek names; this implies that they were chosen deliberately; they could more easily relate to those who were being neglected (McGarvey, *Commentary on Acts*, 106). This doesn't mean however, that these men were prevented from teaching God's word. Philip and Stephen, both, are known to us as faithful preachers of the word.

The spiritual health of a congregation is increased when each Christian seeks an avenue of service. This keeps the Christian on track and focused (and cuts down on complaining; busy Christians are usually happy Christians). And the service rendered will be a blessing to others. When each member of the body is working properly, the body increases. But when work that needs to be done is left to only a few to do, the church will never grow and realize its true potential. You have a gift to use in serving the Lord. Why not find it and use it?

CHAPTER 44

The Preaching of Stephen

"Then the high priest said, 'Are these things so?'"
(Acts 7:1)

This passage refers to the false charges some brought against Stephen. When men from the Synagogue of the Freedmen could not refute Stephen's teaching, they resorted to lies and slander. They found other men who would lie about what Stephen said. This caught the attention of the religious leaders in Jerusalem; they were egged on by another set of accusers. What was their charge? "This man does not cease to speak blasphemous words against this holy place and the law; for we have heard him say that this Jesus of Nazareth will destroy this place and change the customs which Moses delivered to us" (Acts 6:13-14).

Hellenists, Jews who adopted the Greek way of life, would naturally congregate in their respective synagogues. It is likely that Stephen was a Hellenist; this may account for him being one of those chosen to help in the daily distribution of food to the Hellenists/Grecian widows. As such, he would have had an association with a synagogue; maybe at one time he was a member of the synagogue of the Freedmen. As was later true of the Apostle Paul, it would have been natural for Stephen after he became a Christian, to preach in the local synagogues scattered throughout Jerusalem when possible. All of this sets the stage for Acts 7.

The charge of blasphemy against the temple and the Law of Moses was a crime punishable by death. Was this serious charge true? Did Stephen remind his detractors of what Jesus had said many times? "So the Jews answered and said to Him, 'What sign do You show to us, since You do these things?' Jesus answered and said to them, 'Destroy this temple, and in three days I will raise it up,'" (John 2:18-19). Yes, the temple and Judaism would come to an end. Yet, Jesus would provide something better in their place. "Then the Jews said, "It has taken forty-six years to build this temple, and will You raise it up in three days? But He was speaking of the temple of His body" (John 2:20-21). In His glorious resurrection, Jesus made possible His spiritual temple, the church. Jesus claimed to be greater than the temple (Matthew 12:6). What regard did Jesus have for the Law of Moses? "Do not think that I came to destroy the Law or the Prophets. I did not come to destroy but to fulfill. For assuredly, I say to you, till heaven and earth pass away, one jot or one tittle will by no means pass from the law till all is fulfilled" (Matthew 5:17-18).

Today, we do not meet Jesus in or through the Law of Moses or in any remaining vestiges of Judaism. We meet Jesus at the cross. He is the ultimate fulfillment of the Law, the Psalms, and the Prophets. This is what Stephen will tell us in his sermon.

CHAPTER 45

Stephen's Preaching #2

Preaching the gospel is absolutely essential. Jesus said so in His Great Commission (Matthew 28; Mark 16; Luke 24). In a specific way, Jesus entrusted the gospel to the "twelve" apostles; they, under the authority of Christ, went into the entire world carrying the message of salvation. As the early church grew, others became involved in helping carry out the task of spreading the good news. Acts 1:8 provides a "road map" for the work of these early saints. "But you shall receive power when the Holy Spirit has come upon you; and you shall be witnesses to Me in Jerusalem, and in all Judea and Samaria, and to the end of the earth." When we read Acts 6 we find others involved in gospel preaching. We know something about two of these men: Philip and Stephen. Not only was Stephen one of the seven assigned to assist the needy widows, he was also strongly preaching in the synagogues the message of Christ. Instead of accepting Stephen's message, opposition arose in the form of false accusations. Stephen was called to give answer to the Jewish authorities.

"Then the high priest said, 'Are these things so?'" (Acts 7:1). Stephen's answer is a masterful sketch of Old Testament history—a history the Jewish authorities would have been familiar with. Yet, they had failed to learn God's intended lessons. The Old Testament and Stephen's teaching did not dishonor the temple. More than that, the Old Testament and Stephen's teaching pointed all to Jesus Christ, the "Just One" (Acts 7:52). That was the problem. As their fathers had done in rejecting God's prophets, these religious leaders followed suit and rejected the Christ, the greatest prophet of all. Abraham was a key player in the early history of God's people. Beginning in Genesis 12:1-3, Abraham would be the father of a great nation. The general tenor of his life was that of faith. Paul, in Romans 4, uses Abraham as an example of what it means to have saving faith. The Old Testament story moves through Abraham, Isaac, and Jacob. Jacob became the father of 12 sons, the eventual 12 tribes of Israel. Do not miss the big point of this narrative concerning Abraham and his family: The God of glory took the initiative!

God moves from Mesopotamia to Egypt. The story of one of Jacob's sons, Joseph, explains how the 12 tribes, the descendants of Abraham, ended up in Egyptian bondage for 400 years. The land of Egypt did not belong to Israel. They would eventually be delivered. Or, would they? Did they know that one day they would leave bondage?

What is Stephen saying? He is saying that when God makes a promise, He keeps that promise. Stephen points to the ultimate fulfillment of God's promise to save all mankind. That promise was played out in the lives of the Patriarchs. Can it be played out in your life? Read Acts 7 and see.

CHAPTER 46

Stephen's Preaching #3

> "And when forty years had passed, an Angel of the Lord appeared to him in a flame of fire in a bush, in the wilderness of Mount Sinai. When Moses saw it, he marveled at the sight; and as he drew near to observe, the voice of the Lord came to him, saying, 'I am the God of your fathers—the God of Abraham, the God of Isaac, and the God of Jacob.' And Moses trembled and dared not look."
> (Acts 7:30-32)

Stephen's sermon in Acts 7 says much about Moses (Acts 7:17-43). The story of Moses continues the story of God keeping His promise to Abraham. The Israelites, in bondage to Egypt, moaned under the lash of the whip. Moses becomes the key player in Israel's deliverance. Remember that Stephen had been accused of speaking against Moses (Acts 6:14).

Israel was in Egypt for 400 years. Had God forgotten them? No! Exodus 2:24 says, "So God heard their groaning, and God remembered His covenant with Abraham, with Isaac, and with Jacob." When the time was right, Jehovah, the Lord of all history, acted through Moses to deliver Israel. Remember that Abraham would be the father of a great nation; that came true (Exodus 1:9). And remember that God promised to give His people a land to live in. After 40 years under Pharaoh's roof, Moses tried to act on behalf of his people; his initial efforts were rejected. After spending the next 40 years in the wilderness, Moses, the reluctant leader, was called to go before Pharaoh. The Egyptian king refused to let God's people go; he did not respect Jehovah God; yet, God's power would secure the release of the captives. Under the anguished cries of death,

God's people left Egypt. After crossing the Red Sea on dry ground, they moved toward the wilderness; they would soon be in the Promise Land. Or, would they?

"And in their hearts they turned back to Egypt" (Acts 7:39). Israel languished in Egypt for 400 years. Was obedience on their minds? Sadly, their story shows a lack of faith in God. Their hearts were elsewhere. The golden calf incident easily illustrates their failure to recognize God's power and His benevolence toward them. This lack of faith continued into the wilderness; so much so, that finally, the newly released captives from Egypt became captives in the wilderness for 40 years! Stephen quotes from Amos 5, showing that a long-held pattern of rebellion was still present in the hearts of those to whom he preached.

What is Stephen saying to those in Jerusalem, those who rejected the message of salvation through Christ? He is saying to them and to us: We can, if we want to, stand on Holy Ground. Moses did. The Israelites did after constructing the tabernacle and meeting God there for worship. We can stand there today when we submit to the authority of Christ. In our lives, in our families, in our identity as Christ's church, we can stand on holy ground. But we better take our shoes off. How terrible it is to turn away from a Holy God in unholy rebellion.

CHAPTER 47

Stephen's Preaching #4

In the fourth section of Stephen's sermon, the emphasis is on David and Solomon (Acts 7:44-50). The land is settled; the people have a king; the nation of Israel is called to worship at the temple. Stephen makes no pejorative remarks about the temple; this, however, was the charge against him. Acts 6:13-14 says, "They also set up false witnesses who said, 'This man does not cease to speak blasphemous words against this holy place and the law; for we have heard him say that this Jesus of Nazareth will destroy this place and change the customs which Moses delivered to us.'"

Stephen says: What about David and Solomon? These are well-known, great names in the history of God's people. They had a part in building the temple. What then, was the problem?

The religious leaders in Jerusalem made the mistake of elevating the physical, material structure—the temple—over that of Jehovah God, the maker of all things! God does not dwell in temples made with hands. "Thus says the LORD: 'Heaven is My throne, And earth is My footstool. Where is the house that you will build Me? And where is the place of My rest? For all those things My hand has made, And all those things exist,' says the LORD." "But on this one will I look: On him who is poor and of a contrite spirit, And who trembles at My word" (Isaiah 66:1-2). How could God be contained in a man-made dwelling? He moved with Abraham from Ur of the Chaldees to Haran and then to destinations further south. God went with Joseph into Egypt, eventually liberating Israel, and moved them into the Promised Land. God's glory was present in all these locations. Stephen showed more respect for the temple than did his accusers.

What about the Law of Moses? "Then they secretly induced men to say, 'We have heard him speak blasphemous words against Moses and God'" (Acts 6:11). Did Stephen disrespect the Law? Clearly, he had respect for Moses. Moses was rejected by his own people, but not by Stephen. Joseph had been sold into slavery by his brothers. In fact, God's prophets had met a similar fate. Stephen says you have rejected the ultimate, final prophet, Jesus Christ. You have rejected the prophet of prophecy—the one who would be similar to but greater than Moses (Deuteronomy 18:18-20). "You stiff-necked and uncircumcised in heart and ears!" (Acts 7:51). The Jews hated uncircumcised people; but now, that is what they have become in their hearts. They resisted the Holy Spirit of God when they rejected His message as given by the prophets and Stephen and by Jesus. Jesus was no threat to the temple and the Law. He said, "Do not think that I came to destroy the Law or the Prophets. I did not come to destroy but to fulfill" (Matthew 5:17).

Can you imagine the Sanhedrin, a religious body of 70 rabbis, getting out of their seats and rushing in a fever in order to throw stones at Stephen? Can you hear their snarling? Can you hear the gnashing of teeth? Do you see a young man, Saul, holding the coats of his mentors? Yes? No? Maybe we need to see these same things the next time we reject the words of Jesus.

CHAPTER 48

They Stoned Steven

"And they stoned Stephen as he was calling on God and saying, 'Lord Jesus, receive my spirit.' Then he knelt down and cried out with a loud voice, 'Lord, do not charge them with this sin.' And when he had said this, he fell asleep."
(Acts 7:59-60)

Modern day audiences may recoil at the viciousness of the Sanhedrin, the Jewish rulers, 70 in all, who, like wild animals, "gnashed" at Stephen, grinding and gritting their teeth in derision. Their hearts had been opened and were bleeding by the message of Jesus; they stood condemned. Refusing to bow, they continued their opposition to God and His word. How could they have even heard Stephen's message with their ears covered?

Gazing into heaven, Stephen "saw the glory of God, and Jesus standing at the right hand of God." Several passages tell us that Jesus "sits" at the right hand of God, an exalted position (Psalm 110:1; Acts 2:34-35). Here, though, Jesus is standing. Why? F.F. Bruce suggests that "Stephen has been confessing Christ before men, and now he sees Christ confessing his servant before God" (*Acts*, 168). John saw something similar on the isle of Patmos. In one's time of death who better to see than the Lord? Stephen could see the religious rabbis rushing toward him; he could see his accusers—the false witnesses who were required to cast the first stone (Deuteronomy 17:7); he could see a young man named Saul who held the coats of the those laden with rocks; and yes, Stephen could see Jesus!

Stephen prayed, "Lord Jesus, receive my spirit." While on the cross Jesus said, "Father, into Your hands I commit My spirit" (Luke 23:46). This was not all Stephen said, though. His last words were a plea for forgiveness. He "cried out with a loud voice, Lord, do not charge them with this sin." Do you remember Jesus saying, "Father, forgive them, for they do not know what they do" (Luke 23:34). In both deaths, there were false witnesses, there was the charge of blasphemy, and there was a prayer for those who carried out the vile deed. Oh, that we all would emulate our Savior in life and death. Having uttered his last words, this faithful preacher "fell asleep." This tragic death ends with peaceful words.

We talk about Stephen the "first Christian martyr." That is not what Luke emphasizes. Luke helps us understand that Stephen's message about the Law of Moses and the temple found ultimate fulfillment in Jesus. Even after Solomon finished the temple, Jehovah made it clear that He did not "dwell in temples made with hands." The message of Acts is that a resurrected Jesus, as promised, would be with His faithful people—Stephen who lost his life because of his preaching—men and women who were driven from home by persecution, but were driven to preach because of Jesus. "The church" is not buildings; the church is people. God's word is His word—not the traditions of men. God's word must not be imprisoned by a lack of faith. His word must go forth even when facing the threat of persecution. We don't want to be stoned with stones do we? But are we willing to live within the purview of God's word and His providence, believing that His ways are best? We might be willing to live that way; are we prepared to die that way?

CHAPTER 49

Philip the Evangelist

Stephen was stoned to death; Saul persecuted God's people; the church went forth preaching the word; Philip proclaimed Christ to the Samaritans. So begins Acts chapter eight. God's people would not be silenced; God's church would not be destroyed; the blood of martyrs paved a trail for the unfolding of salvation through Christ. "Nor is there salvation in any other, for there is no other name under heaven given among men by which we must be saved" (Acts 4:12).

Acts 8:5: "Then Philip went down to the city of Samaria and preached Christ to them." Philip the evangelist was "heralding" the gospel; he openly, publicly proclaimed the good news of Jesus. New Testament Christians were evangelizing; their message was *the evangel*—the good news of salvation. The word was preached (Acts 8:4); scripture was preached (Acts 8:35); the word of the Lord was preached (Acts 8:25). Stephen's death brought persecution; it also brought dispersion; it also brought the seed of the kingdom to those beyond the confines of Jerusalem. Acts chapter eight fills in the outline of Acts 1:8: "You shall be witnesses to Me in Jerusalem, and in all Judea and Samaria, and to the end of the earth."

Acts 8:12 tells us what Philip preached. "But when they believed Philip as he preached the things concerning the kingdom of God and the name of Jesus Christ, both men and women were baptized." The gospel is God's power to salvation (Romans 1:16); clearly, the Samaritans believed this eternal truth. Soon they turned away from Simon with his sorcery, tricks, and deceptions, seeing clearly the difference between Simon's works and the works of the Holy Spirit of God as shown by Philip. They could see the power in Philip's message; His message was true as demonstrated by the power of God. They believed Philip's message for what it was (and is)—God's message of salvation. No longer were they deceived by Simon.

You may believe most anything you want to believe. Only when you believe the glad tidings of Jesus and obey that message, can you be saved from sin. You might believe in Simon's message; you might believe in some other message. But only when you believe and obey Christ's message can you be free from sin. Essential elements of Philip's sermon included the kingdom—the rule of God in the hearts of men, the name of Jesus Christ—His authority as expressed in His word, and baptism—water baptism by or in the name of Christ (by His authority). No longer would the Samaritans be held captive by a false, damning message; they were now set free by the good news of Jesus.

Preaching in the name of Jesus includes the totality of all He taught men and women to believe and obey. Certainly the Samaritans repented of their sins (Acts 2:38). Certainly they were baptized (Acts 2:38). Certainly they were saved by grace through faith. Certainly their hearts were pricked by the message they heard (Acts 2:37). One more important element is seen in the conversion of the Samaritans. Acts 8:6: "And the multitudes with one accord heeded the things spoken by Philip, hearing and seeing the miracles which he did." They *heeded* Philip's message. They listened. They paid attention. They took the message into their hearts. They were converted, truly converted to the Lord. Have you listened? Are you converted to the Lord?

CHAPTER 50

Simon the Sorcerer

"But there was a certain man called Simon, who previously practiced sorcery in the city and astonished the people of Samaria, claiming that he was someone great, to whom they all gave heed, from the least to the greatest, saying, 'This man is the great power of God.'"
(Acts 8:9-10)

There have always been challenges to the gospel of Christ. We rejoice with the 3,000 on the day of Pentecost, but undoubtedly thousands of others resisted the call of the gospel. When Paul preached to the citizens of Athens (Acts 17), some were interested, some mocked, and some put off listening until another time. The convenient season (Acts 24:25) came for some; for others, it never came.

When Philip went to Samaria to preach, he found people, great and small, who were under the influence of a sorcerer named Simon. Simon's deceptions were such that the people viewed him as a deity of some kind. Soon, though, a change took place in Simon. He heard Philip's message and was baptized. Philip was joined by two apostles, Peter and John, who came to help mature these new Christians through the working of the Holy Spirit. When Simon saw what the apostles did, he wanted to have the same power:

"And when Simon saw that through the laying on of the apostles' hands the Holy Spirit was given, he offered them money, saying, 'Give me this power also, that anyone on whom I lay hands may receive the Holy Spirit,'" (Acts 8:18-19). Simon's request brought an immediate rebuke from Peter. Simon's heart was not right in the matter; he was told to repent in order to be forgiven. Some argue that Simon was not a true believer in the first place; therefore, it is not possible that a baptized believer, a true child of God, can actually fall from grace. Luke tells us that "Simon himself also believed" (Acts 8:13). If he was not a true believer and if he did not sincerely repent, then he was not a fit subject for scriptural baptism in the first place. That would not, however, invalidate the true purpose of baptism in the name of Jesus Christ. Simon *also* believed; he, with other Samaritans, believed and obeyed the gospel. If he only pretended to believe, then Luke's account, which we take at face value, is suspect. If Simon was hopelessly doomed to damnation, then Peter's words are nonsense. Acts 8:22: "Repent therefore of this your wickedness, and pray God if perhaps the thought of your heart may be forgiven you." Peter did not say that Simon's heart never was right. He said repent and forgiveness will come.

Instead of trying to circumvent Bible teaching about salvation, why not rejoice that one can hear and believe and obey the gospel and be saved from sin? Rather than trying to say one can never fall from grace, why not recognize the possibility and be thankful that when (if) we do fall, we can repent and be restored to the Lord? Even if we end up like Simon, full of bitterness and iniquity, we can come back to the Lord and walk with Him once more. We must remember, though, that perhaps the greatest challenge to the gospel, the greatest obstacle to being right with the Lord, is SELF. Greed, wickedness, pride—these sins and more can get hold of us, thwarting the intent of the gospel. *"Alas! What hourly dangers rise! What snares beset my way! To Heaven, oh! let me lift my eyes, And hourly watch and pray."*

CHAPTER 51

The Ethiopian Eunuch

"Now an angel of the Lord spoke to Philip, saying, 'Arise and go toward the south along the road which goes down from Jerusalem to Gaza.'"
(Acts 8:26)

After Philip preached to the Samaritans, he moved in a southwest direction, climbing over the Judean Mountain, and headed toward the Mediterranean Sea. His destination was Gaza, which was located in a desert place; rather than dry and arid, this place was sparsely populated. Philip didn't bask in the glow of recent successes; rather, when the angel told him to go, "he arose and went" (Acts 8:27). People today say: "Well, if an angel told me to do something, I would quickly obey." What if the Lord told you to do something? Would His words mean more to you than an angel? God's will in these last days is revealed through Jesus Christ. "God, who at various times and in various ways spoke in time past to the fathers by the prophets, has in these last days spoken to us by His Son" (Hebrews 1:1-2). Don't wait for an angel to speak to you. Read the Bible and do what it says.

You never know who you might run into in the desert. Philip came upon a eunuch from Ethiopia. This man could have been a Gentile who had converted to Judaism—a proselyte; he may have been a Jew; the Jewish dispersion had permeated into Africa (read Isaiah 56:3-4). He worked for the queen as her treasurer—he was a man of power and influence. He was dedicated to what he believed—he traveled a long way from home in order to worship. He was educated; he was able to read Isaiah the prophet. Was he sincere? How can we doubt his sincerity? Was he honest and genuine in his religion? Sincerity is good, but sincerity alone is not enough. We can be sincerely mistaken. The eunuch was a worshiper; that is good, but acceptable worship must comport with God's word. He needed to hear more about the Jesus which Isaiah spoke about.

Philip obeyed the instructions not only of the angel, but also of the Holy Spirit. "Then the Spirit said to Philip, 'Go near and overtake this chariot,'" (Acts 8:29). Again, Philip obeyed—he "ran" to meet the chariot. Philip asked, "Do you understand what you are reading?" The Ethiopian didn't try to bluff his way out of the situation. He said, "How can I, unless someone guides me?" And he asked Philip to come up and sit with him."

Isaiah 53 is a highpoint of Scripture. Isaiah points us to the Suffering Servant, the Messiah, the Christ of God. Isaiah 53 argues for the deity of Christ; it argues for the inspiration of God's word. It speaks of salvation. "Of this salvation the prophets have inquired and searched carefully, who prophesied of the grace that would come to you" (1 Peter 1:10). Yet, the Eunuch asked, "Of whom does the prophet say this, of himself or of some other man?"

Imagine the eunuch and Philip riding along in the chariot (surely a bumpy ride), with the Isaiah scroll unfurled before them. They ponder Isaiah's word about a lamb being led to the slaughter. Could this be the Messiah? No! The Jews were not looking for a Messiah that suffered. Yet, Jesus the Lamb of God, applied Isaiah 53 to Himself (Luke 22:37; Isaiah 53:12). The eunuch heard many things while in Jerusalem. It was not until he was on his way home that he heard the words he needed to hear: "Then Philip opened his mouth, and beginning at this Scripture, preached Jesus to him" (Acts 8:35).

CHAPTER 52

The Ethiopian Eunuch #2

> "Then Philip opened his mouth, and beginning at this Scripture, preached Jesus to him. Now as they went down the road, they came to some water. And the eunuch said, 'See, here is water. What hinders me from being baptized?' Then Philip said, 'If you believe with all your heart, you may.' And he answered and said, 'I believe that Jesus Christ is the Son of God.'"
> (Acts 8:35-37)

What do we talk about when we open our mouths? The weather? Baseball? Our jobs? Our families? Jesus said, "Out of the abundance of the heart the mouth speaks. A good man out of the good treasure of his heart brings forth good things, and an evil man out of the evil treasure brings forth evil things. But I say to you that for every idle word men may speak, they will give account of it in the day of judgment" (Matthew 12:35-37). Can we agree that today, in the Lord's church, we need more people who will talk about Jesus? Remember that Philip preached Christ to the Samaritans (Acts 8:5). Now Luke says that Philip preached "Jesus." Beginning from Scripture, Isaiah 53, he preached the gospel to the man from Ethiopia. If you are going to open your mouth and preach from Scripture as Philip did, then Jesus is the only thing you can preach. A dominant theme in the book of Acts is the coming of the Spirit (Acts 2:17ff; Joel 2:28-32); this was something the Old Testament prophets anticipated (Jeremiah 31:31-34; Ezekiel 36:24-26); it was in obedience to the Spirit of God that Philip went to the eunuch. The twin themes of suffering and resurrection are featured often in Luke's history. When the apostles were threatened, beaten, and cast into prison, they were suffering for the cause of Christ. The Messiah, as Isaiah 53 says, suffered for all, including the eunuch. Soon, Philip and the eunuch came upon a certain body of water. "Now as they went down the road, they came to some water. And the eunuch said, 'See, here is water. What hinders me from being baptized?'" (Acts 8:36). Why did he ask this question? Is there anything specific in Isaiah 53 about baptism? The answer is that he learned from Philip's preaching that this is what the Savior wanted him to do. When we open our mouths and do not preach the necessity of baptism for the forgiveness of sins, we are not preaching the same Jesus that Philip preached.

Was faith involved in the conversion of the eunuch? Acts 8:37 says, "Then Philip said, 'If you believe with all your heart, you may.' And he answered and said, 'I believe that Jesus Christ is the Son of God.'" The people on the Day of Pentecost had faith in Jesus (Acts 2:37). The Samaritans had faith (Acts 8:12). Water baptism for the remission of sins comports with God's word, only when the person seeking salvation acts in faith, repents of sin, and confesses the name of Christ. When the eunuch said "I believe," Philip knew that he understood what he was hearing, believing, and doing. Then, and only then, did Philip baptize the eunuch.

"Now when they came up out of the water, the Spirit of the Lord caught Philip away, so that the eunuch saw him no more; and he went on his way rejoicing" (Acts 8:39). Do you want to be truly happy? Acknowledge Jesus as the Christ of God, the Messiah. Listen to God's word. Believe it and obey it. When you do this you can rejoice. You rejoice not because you think you did the Lord's will; you rejoice because you know you obeyed the Lord's will. And now, as you go on your way, as you open your mouth, you, too, will "preach Jesus."

CHAPTER 53

Saul of Tarsus

Notable conversions get our attention. The Samaritans, viewed by many as unlikely candidates for salvation, heard Philip's preaching and became followers of Jesus. How likely was it that a man from Ethiopia would meet a preacher and then hear him "preach Jesus" beginning from the very passage the Ethiopian had been reading—a passage from the Old Testament of all places? However, can there be a case of conversion, that above all others, always gets our attention? Is there someone in the New Testament who, after hearing God's word, changed his or her life to the extent that we shake our heads in wonder? Are we incredulous that an avowed enemy of the cross could change the direction of his life and become the world-famous Apostle Paul? The answer "yes" can be given to all these questions.

It seems obvious that the conversion of Saul of Tarsus is important to Luke's story of the early church. The historian gives us three different accounts of the same conversion (Acts 9, 22, 26). Is Saul's Damascus Road experience typical of conversion to Christ in this day and age; is it the norm for people today? Or, is Saul's conversion exceptional and unusual? Some of the events were certainly dramatic and supernatural (lighting, voice from heaven). Paul (his name later) said that he saw the Lord. "Then last of all He was seen by me also, as by one born out of due time" (1 Corinthians 15:8). Why not, though, distinguish between the outward, dramatic elements of Paul's conversion and the inner, essential elements that still apply to all today? Paul wrote to Timothy saying, "And I thank Christ Jesus our Lord who has enabled me, because He counted me faithful, putting me into the ministry, although I was formerly a blasphemer, a persecutor, and an insolent man; but I obtained mercy because I did it ignorantly in unbelief" (1 Timothy 1:12-13). Why not be thankful that the Lord was patient with Paul? Instead of trying to circumvent some element of Bible teaching, why not be thankful that the Lord is patient with us, too?

"Then Saul, still breathing threats and murder against the disciples of the Lord, went to the high priest and asked letters from him to the synagogues of Damascus, so that if he found any who were of the Way, whether men or women, he might bring them bound to Jerusalem" (Acts 9:1-2). Clearly, Saul was doing all he could do to get rid Jesus' followers. Saul was persecuting the followers of Christ; in doing so, he was persecuting Jesus. Saul went from holding the coats of the murderers of Stephen, to using all the religious and political muscle possible to oppose the Lord's people. He was "still" looking for opportunities to assail these early disciples. The persecuted Christians went forth preaching the word (Acts 8:4); some undoubtedly were "scattered" to Damascus. And now Saul is looking for them. His hatred and hostility were unabated. He had *carte blanche* from the leaders of the synagogues to round up all who were of "the Way." Like a ravenous dog, he pursued his prey.

How could someone, anyone, so disposed, listen to the gospel? Paul later said, "And I punished them often in every synagogue and compelled them to blaspheme; and being exceedingly enraged against them, I persecuted them even to foreign cities" (Acts 26:11). You do not want to meet Saul anywhere. But he soon met someone on the road to Damascus. And his life was never the same. That is notable!

CHAPTER 54

Saul Meets Jesus

> "As he journeyed he came near Damascus, and suddenly a light shone around him from heaven. Then he fell to the ground, and heard a voice saying to him, 'Saul, Saul, why are you persecuting Me?' And he said, 'Who are You, Lord?' Then the Lord said, 'I am Jesus, whom you are persecuting. It is hard for you to kick against the goads.'"
> (Acts 9:3-5)

Saul's journey from Jerusalem to Damascus would have taken at least five days, maybe six. Still, the distance of 150 miles did not stop Saul from his intended purpose in life—to get rid of all the followers of Jesus Christ. The persecutor who later turned preacher, told King Agrippa, "I punished them often in every synagogue and compelled them to blaspheme; and being exceedingly enraged against them, I persecuted them even to foreign cities" (Acts 26:11). While Damascus was an idyllic city in an oasis surrounded by desert, Saul intended to fill its streets with the blood of Christians. But he met someone who forever changed his life.

A light brighter than the noonday sun blinded Saul, knocking him to the ground. Now, for the first time, this avowed enemy of Jesus falls before his Savior. Hearing a voice in the Hebrew language, Saul can only ask: Who are you? The voice was personal; it spoke to Saul. "I am Jesus, whom you are persecuting." Saul's response is easily understood; he trembled in astonishment and then asked: "What do you want me to do?" After being told what to do, Saul did exactly that.

The big question in this story is: Why did the Lord visibly and audibly appear to Saul of Tarsus? We say: to convert him; to save him. And surely this would be true and in line with the purpose for which Jesus came to this earth—namely, to die on the cross for the sins of mankind, including Saul. If this is so, and there is not some other consideration in the matter, then the Lord did something for Saul's salvation that He has not done for any other person. Yes, Jesus wanted Saul to be saved; Jesus wants all people to be saved. But in Saul's case of conversion, there seems to be more to the story.

"But rise and stand on your feet; for I have appeared to you for this purpose, to make you a minister and a witness both of the things which you have seen and of the things which I will yet reveal to you. I will deliver you from the Jewish people, as well as from the Gentiles, to whom I now send you, to open their eyes, in order to turn them from darkness to light, and from the power of Satan to God, that they may receive forgiveness of sins and an inheritance among those who are sanctified by faith in Me" (Acts 26:16-18). Jesus wanted Saul to be His chosen ambassador to the Gentiles. Jesus wanted Saul to testify that the Savior was indeed alive. To so testify, Saul needed to see the risen Lord. "Then last of all He was seen by me also" (1 Corinthians 15:8).

The fact that Saul heard and saw the Lord (a miraculous event) is not necessary for the conversion of sinners today. Listening for voices and looking for visions will only bring disappointment and disillusionment. Saul asked: "What do you want me to do?" When he received the answer, he obeyed. Saul did not say that what he experienced was enough to save him. He told Agrippa: "I was not disobedient to the heavenly vision" (Acts 26:19). Will you do what Saul did and be saved from sin?

CHAPTER 55

Saul and Ananias

"Now there was a certain disciple at Damascus named Ananias; and to him the Lord said in a vision, 'Ananias.' And he said, 'Here I am, Lord.'"
(Acts 9:10)

While we recognize Saul's intense hatred for the followers of Jesus, his complete devotion to what he believed was right, and his evident sincerity and good conscience, still he lacked what the Lord was offering—salvation through the blood of Christ. Fasting and praying might indicate a change of direction, but still, Saul needed to come in contact with the Lord's will for his life.

The book of Acts indicates that when someone needed to hear the gospel, the gospel was presented to that person by a "preacher." The gospel is communicated by a messenger. "How beautiful are the feet of those who preach the gospel of peace, who bring glad tidings of good things!" (Romans 10:15). So, Ananias is summoned. Ananias, at first, was reluctant to go to Saul. Who can blame him? Saul's reputation as a violent persecutor of God's people was well known. When the Lord insisted, Ananias went to Saul. "Brother Saul," a common greeting, was not a statement about Saul's spiritual condition, yea or nay. Saul could not see; maybe Ananias wanted to convey warmth and good will to this blind persecutor. This meeting resulted in the scales falling from Saul's eyes and his baptism (presumably by Ananias). Only then did Saul eat some food.

"Then Saul spent some days with the disciples at Damascus. Immediately he preached the Christ in the synagogues, that He is the Son of God.

Then all who heard were amazed and said, "Is this not he who destroyed those who called on this name in Jerusalem, and has come here for that purpose, so that he might bring them bound to the chief priests?" (Acts 9:19-21). While the Christians in Damascus were naturally skeptical about the change in Saul, it is clear that he was soon accepted into the fellowship of believers.

When Saul obeyed the gospel, he was added to the Lord's church (Acts 2:47). His relationship to Christ changed. No longer was Saul a persecutor; as he preached Christ, he was often persecuted for this radical change. Saul immediately began doing what the Lord wanted him to do; he preached that Jesus was the Christ, the Messiah, the Christ of God. He argued about who Jesus was; he appealed to the Old Testament in support of his preaching; he increased in strength and courage. Imagine the surprise of the authorities in the synagogues—those who had granted him approval to kill Christians—as Saul now worked with the followers of Christ.

Following Jesus always comes with a price. "But their plot became known to Saul. And they watched the gates day and night, to kill him. Then the disciples took him by night and let him down through the wall in a large basket" (Acts 9:24-25). Saul openly traveled the road to Damascus, pursuing Jesus' disciples. Now, he leaves Damascus under the cover of night in order to escape with his life. Paul wrote to Timothy: "All who desire to live godly in Christ Jesus will suffer persecution" (2 Timothy 3:12). Paul wrote to the Philippians: "For to me, to live is Christ, and to die is gain" (Philippians 1:21). Are you on the Damascus Road?

CHAPTER 56

Cornelius

> "There was a certain man in Caesarea called Cornelius, a centurion of what was called the Italian Regiment, a devout man and one who feared God with all his household, who gave alms generously to the people, and prayed to God always."
> (Acts 10:1-2)

God's plan for all men to be saved began with the Jews, His chosen people, the vehicle through whom the Messiah came. The gospel went to the "Jew first" and then later to the Greeks. It was a matter of prophecy that Gentiles could be part of the kingdom. Amos 9:11-12 says, "On that day I will raise up the tabernacle of David, which has fallen down, and repair its damages; I will raise up its ruins, and rebuild it as in the days of old; that they may possess the remnant of Edom, and all the Gentiles who are called by My name, says the LORD who does this thing." In Acts 15 when Paul and the leaders in Jerusalem discussed whether circumcision and other aspects of Moses' law should be bound on Gentiles, James quoted from Amos, making it clear that Gentiles could indeed come to the Lord (and circumcision was not binding on the Gentiles). Rehearsing the events in Acts 10, Peter said, "Then God has also granted to the Gentiles repentance to life" (Acts 11:18). When Jesus died, "the middle wall of separation" was broken down. All, Jew and Gentile alike, could be one in Christ.

But why would a devout man who feared God (along with his household) need converting in the first place? Who was Cornelius? He was a military man, commanding 100 men; in this, he worked for the Roman government—something that constantly raised the ire of the Jews in Palestine. Yet, this "just man" had "a good reputation among all the nation of the Jews" (Acts 10:22). With Italy in his background, Cornelius would have been exposed to the pagan influences of Roman and Greek culture. Being in Palestine, though, he would have had opportunity to see Jews worshiping and sacrificing according to the Law of Moses. Was Cornelius a proselyte—a convert to Judaism? It seems clear that he had turned away from any or all early influences and at some point attempted to serve the living and true God.

Luke tells us that Cornelius "feared God." Was he a religious man? It seems so. Acts 10:35 says, "But in every nation whoever fears Him and works righteousness is accepted by Him." Did he fear God in this sense—that is, was he serving God according to the gospel that Peter was preaching to him? If so, why was Peter sent to Cornelius in the first place to speak "words by which you and all your household will be saved" (Acts 11:14)? Later in Acts, Paul spoke to "Men of Israel, and you who fear God" and to "Sons of the family of Abraham, and those among you who fear God" (Acts 13:16, 26). Often, uncircumcised Gentiles "feared God" and attended synagogue services, but they were excluded from full participation in Judaism. They were sometimes referred to as "proselyte(s) of the gate." Gentiles could come close to the temple, but not too close.

Cornelius, even though a good man who did lots of good things, was a lost man. That is why Peter was sent to him. God wants all to be saved; Jesus died for all. While Cornelius served God according to all the "light" he had, he still needed the full light of the message of Christ's gospel. So do we.

CHAPTER 57

Peter's Sermon to Cornelius

An angel appeared to Cornelius. Peter was entranced by a vision. Men from Caesarea came to Peter inviting him to preach to Cornelius. Peter, who had doubts about the Gentiles, went anyway the very next day, answering the Lord's call. The Holy Spirit was involved in Cornelius' conversion. How do you describe these happenings? Amazing, strange, or, counterintuitive? Whatever our reactions may be, remember that Cornelius was still not in Christ. He may have been on his way to the Lord. He worshiped God. He was generous; his reputation was sound. Still, he needed a preacher to communicate God's message of salvation through Christ to him.

What were "the points" of Peter's sermon? First, "You know how unlawful it is for a Jewish man to keep company with or go to one of another nation. But God has shown me that I should not call any man common or unclean" (Acts 10:28). While it was *taboo* for a Jew to enter into the house of a Gentile, Peter was beginning to understand that "the blessed gospel is for all." Verse 34 says, "I perceive that God shows no partiality." When the Apostle John tells us that Jesus died for the "world" (John 3:16), we know that includes Cornelius. It also includes you and me.

The second point is, "But in every nation whoever fears Him and works righteousness is accepted by Him" (Acts 10:35). Peter, a Jew, now knows that the Mosaic Covenant is not the basis for salvation. Every person who will *fear* God—respect Him in every way, and *work righteousness*—yield to heaven's will—can be saved. God does not respect nations; He respects character of heart. People are not arbitrarily chosen for salvation or damnation. Those who *will come can come* and be saved.

The third point is, "The word which God sent to the children of Israel, preaching peace through Jesus Christ—He is Lord of all" (Acts 10:36). Jesus is Lord and Master; all who come to Him, seeking the peace only He can give, will recognize that He is preeminent in all things. Interestingly, Peter says, "*That word you know*, which was proclaimed throughout all Judea, and began from Galilee...how God anointed Jesus of Nazareth... who went about doing good and healing all who were oppressed by the devil...And we are witnesses of all things which He did both in the land of the Jews and in Jerusalem, whom they killed by hanging on a tree" (Acts 10:37-40). What did Cornelius "know?" How did he know these things? Peter's "witness" to Jesus summarizes the salient facts of Jesus' life—namely, the death, burial, and resurrection. What the Jews did to Jesus, and what Jesus did when He walked the dusty roads in Palestine were well-attested to. While Cornelius and those with him may have had some knowledge about Jesus of Nazareth, they still did not know or fully understand their specific need for the salvation that only Jesus could give.

The fourth point is, "And He commanded us to preach to the people, and to testify that it is He who was ordained by God to be Judge of the living and the dead. To Him all the prophets witness that, through His name, whoever believes in Him will receive remission of sins" (Acts 10:42-43). What happened after the sermon was over? Stay tuned.

CHAPTER 58

Peter's Sermon to Cornelius #2

"While Peter was still speaking these words, the Holy Spirit fell upon all those who heard the word. And those of the circumcision who believed were astonished, as many as came with Peter, because the gift of the Holy Spirit had been poured out on the Gentiles also. For they heard them speak with tongues and magnify God. Then Peter answered, 'Can anyone forbid water, that these should not be baptized who have received the Holy Spirit just as we have?' And he commanded them to be baptized in the name of the Lord. Then they asked him to stay a few days."
(Acts 10:44-48)

What did the outpouring of the Holy Spirit actually do for Cornelius and his household? Did the Holy Spirit give them faith? In Acts 15 Peter discussed the events of Acts 10 and said, "Men and brethren, you know that a good while ago God chose among us, that by my mouth the Gentiles should hear the word of the gospel and believe" (Acts 15:7). It was through the testimony of Peter, the preaching of the gospel, that Cornelius and his household could come to believe in Jesus. Romans 10:17 says, "So then faith comes by hearing, and hearing by the word of God." Did the Holy Spirit give Cornelius a clean, pure heart that would enable him to accept the gospel? Acts 15:8-9 says, "So God, who knows the heart, acknowledged them by giving them the Holy Spirit, just as He did to us, and made no distinction between us and them, purifying their hearts by faith." Their hearts were cleansed by faith, by the hearing and acceptance of the gospel, not by a miraculous gift of the Holy Spirit. Acts 11:14 says that Peter would tell Cornelius "words by which you and all your household will be saved." Did the giving of the Holy Spirit mean that the sins of Cornelius were forgiven? Acts 10:43 says, "To Him all the prophets witness that, through His name, whoever believes in Him will receive remission of sins." God forgives sin when men and women come to Him in faith—faith that is prepared to accept His message and obey it. That forgiveness is through the blood of Christ, through faith—faith used here in a comprehensive sense—it is used for the totality of God's divine will for the alien sinner—not "salvation by faith alone."

Was the giving of the Holy Spirit to Cornelius and his household evidence of their pardon from sin? Acts 11:15 says, "And as I began to speak, the Holy Spirit fell upon them, as upon us at the beginning." *I* refers to Peter; *them* refers to Cornelius and his household; *us* refers to the Apostles; *at the beginning* refers to the Day of Pentecost. On that day the Apostles, by the power of the Spirit, preached the gospel, using languages they had not known previously. That is what Cornelius did. "For they heard them speak with tongues and magnify God" (Acts 10:46). Why? Peter recognized the purpose of the outpouring of the Holy Spirit on the Gentiles. He said, "Can anyone forbid water, that these should not be baptized who have received the Holy Spirit just as we have?" (Acts 10:47).

The Holy Spirit confirmed Peter's preaching that all men could be saved. The Holy Spirit confirmed that the Gentiles could be saved. Was Cornelius compelled irresistibly to obey the gospel? No. Did he have a choice to make? Yes. Did he have free will to exercise? Yes. He heard the gospel, believed it, and obeyed it. And now the gospel is going forth into "all the world."

CHAPTER 59

Christians in Antioch

"So it was that for a whole year they assembled with the church and taught a great many people. And the disciples were first called Christians in Antioch."
(Acts 11:26)

Even though the matter of Gentiles being accepted into the kingdom without circumcision was not yet settled completely (at least in the minds of many Jews) the gospel preached by men such as Barnabas and Paul continued to produce good results. Peter opened the door for the Gentiles; now they are hearing and accepting God's word (Acts 11:20). Repercussions from the stoning of Stephen were still being felt (Acts 11:19); but these dedicated saints continued to reach out to all who would listen. The fact that preachers from Cyprus and Cyrene came to Antioch to work indicates the further expansion of the kingdom. "And the hand of the Lord was with them, and a great number believed and turned to the Lord" (Acts 11:21). These early saints were doing what Jesus said to do: "You shall be witnesses to Me in Jerusalem, and in all Judea and Samaria, and to the end of the earth" (Acts 1:8). The Apostles may have led the way; many others joined in. Geographical and cultural expansion was taking place.

Acts 11:22 says, "Then news of these things came to the ears of the church in Jerusalem, and they sent out Barnabas to go as far as Antioch." Indicating approval of the conversion of the Gentiles, the church in Jerusalem (presumably the elders), wanted Barnabas to travel to Antioch in order to teach and encourage these new Christians. The same thing happened earlier in Luke's narrative (Acts 8:14). Barnabas, the "Son of Encouragement" (Acts 4:36), has been called "the man with the biggest heart in the church" (Barclay as quoted in *Acts*, Stott, 203). When Barnabas got to Antioch (estimated population of 500,000 in the first century) what did he find? He found people who had been exposed to and continued to benefit from the "grace of God" (Acts 11:23). You can see the grace of God in lives that have been changed by the gospel. The *encourager encouraged* the new Christians to continue in wholehearted service to the Lord. Soon, many others joined the number of saints. Saul (not Paul until Acts 13:13) joined Barnabas in the work of preaching. We are not surprised to hear that Barnabas was willing to share the "limelight" with Saul. Together, along with the church, they met together, worshiped, studied, and grew.

Who were these people? Acts 6:1 says they were "disciples." Acts 9:2 says they were people of "the Way." Acts 9:13 says they were "saints." Acts 9:30 says they were "brethren." Acts 10:45 says they were "believers." Acts 11:26 says they were "Christians." They were marked, identified, and recognized as people of Jesus Christ, the Messiah. The designation *Christian* is a powerful one. *Christian* provokes ire, anger, persecution, and derision. *Christian*, in the minds and hearts and lives of true believers, evokes joy, happiness, and thankfulness. It identifies who and what the people of God are—people who hear and obey the gospel. All that we are and ever hope to be is because of Jesus Christ. Let us wear His name.

CHAPTER 60

A Praying Church

"Peter was therefore kept in prison, but constant prayer was offered to God for him by the church."
(Acts 12:5)

Conversions, success, rejoicing—Luke's story about these early Christians buoys our faith and hope; if they could serve the Lord in the face of great opposition, then maybe we, too, can be the people of Christ—Christians! Their faith was in the Lord. They could remember the words of Jesus: "I am with you always, even to the end of the age" (Matthew 28:20). But sadness enters the picture in Acts 12.

"Now about that time Herod the king stretched out his hand to harass some from the church. Then he killed James the brother of John with the sword. And because he saw that it pleased the Jews, he proceeded further to seize Peter also. Now it was during the Days of Unleavened Bread" (Acts 12:1-3). This ruler, Herod Agrippa I, was the grandson of Herod the Great. He ruled in Palestine under the umbrellas of Caligula and Claudius, friends and schoolmates from the past. Herod Agrippa's uncle was Antipas, the man who put Jesus on trial (Luke 23:7). He was also the nephew of Herod the Tetrarch, the man who beheaded John the Baptist. Herod Agrippa was anxious to preserve the peace in Palestine; always hoping to avoid raising the ire of Rome. Often in Acts the Jews sought to persecute the Christians. Now an official joins the fray. The work of God hit an obstacle; James is dead, the first apostle to suffer martyrdom.

The Feast of Unleavened Bread came immediately after Passover. During this time Jewish law did not allow trials or sentencing of any offender.

So Peter was put in prison; a trial and death were soon to come. Clearly, Herod did not want Peter to escape; four squads of soldiers (sixteen in all) were assigned to guard this "notorious fisherman." Was the situation hopeless? What will happen to Peter? How can these Christians resist the mighty power of Rome? There were two powers at work. Rome had political and military might; God's people had faith and prayer. What did the Christians do?

They prayed. Did they remember that earlier, after John and Peter were released from prison, that they prayed to God (Acts 4:23ff)? Soon the apostles were imprisoned again, only to have an angel release them from their jail cells (Acts 5:19). Would that happen this time? Whatever they may have remembered, their prayers now "were constant." They were following the Lord's example when He was in Gethsemane. Luke 22:44 says, "And being in agony, He prayed more earnestly."

Luke doesn't say if Peter was experiencing any anxiety about being in jail. Was Peter a "sound sleeper?" How did sleep come when he was tied to two soldiers? Again, an angel stepped in, releasing Peter from his bonds. Peter said this is the Lord's will; "The Lord sent His angel" (Acts 12:11). At Mary's house, many were still praying. Specifically, what did they pray for? Luke doesn't tell us. Did they pray that Peter would have a peaceful time to die? Did they pray for his release? We may wonder about their reaction to Peter's sudden appearance. Whatever our musings might be, the church was praying, Peter was alive, and the gospel continued to go forth. "The word of God grew and multiplied" (Acts 12:24).

CHAPTER 61

The Voice of a God, Not of a Man

> "So on a set day Herod, arrayed in royal apparel, sat on his throne and gave an oration to them. And the people kept shouting, 'The voice of a god and not of a man'!" Then immediately an angel of the Lord struck him, because he did not give glory to God. And he was eaten by worms and died."
> (Acts 12:21-23)

Peter was now at large; Herod was still in charge. Seeking to escape the unpleasantness of living in Jerusalem, the ruler traveled to Caesarea, the provincial capital. A dispute about the acquisition of needed food stuffs resulted in a meeting between Herod and his neighbors from Tyre and Sidon (sea coast cities). Enlisting the help of Herod's personal aide, Blastus, the parties in the dispute came before the king. Herod arrives; predictably, the people cry, "The voice of a god and not of a man!"

Josephus' *Antiquities XIX* adds some detail to Luke's account. Josephus tells us that the sun glistened brightly on Herod's silver robe. The people shout in deference to Herod. The king accepted their worship; they said and he let them say, "You are a god, not a man!" It is one thing to be flattered without asking for such; it is another thing to accept accolades that can only rightly belong to Almighty God. Luke says, "He did not give glory to God." Then, "An angel of the Lord struck him…and he was eaten by worms and died." Josephus tells us that Herod developed a great pain in his stomach; he was then carried to his palace and died five days later.

When men and women, regardless of whom they might be (presidents, the Supreme Court, public opinion) usurp the honor that is due to God, judgment is certain. How sad that we will not let God be God; we will not recognize that we are clay in the hands of the potter. In Herod's case, judgment was sudden. Whether the Lord comes soon or lingers, judgment is sure. Herod appeared before his subjects "on a set day." Another *set day* is coming and all will stand before the judge of all the earth. Israel of old "rose early offered burnt offerings, and brought peace offerings; and the people sat down to eat and drink, and rose up to play" (Exodus 32:6). The golden calf was a poor substitute for God. Our culture does the same. We substitute our will for God's will. We believe that whatever makes us happy is God's will (if one even seeks any justification). The line between right and wrong is blurred, not by God, but by those who "have idols in their hearts" (Ezekiel 14:4).

Herod in his arrogance believed he was above all. Herod the tyrant and murderer was dead. "But the word of God grew and multiplied" (Acts 12:24). Is there a lesson for us today? Herod goes on a rampage, killing James, seeking Peter's life, persecuting the church. Yet, God is more powerful; God is able to triumph over all human powers and governments. While the persecution of these early Christians certainly was not pleasant (an understatement), in the end the empires and pronouncements of men will crumble. The kingdom of God will stand, but only when we listen to God and not to man.

CHAPTER 62

The Church at Antioch

After delivering aid to the churches in Judea (Jerusalem included among them Acts 11:29), Barnabas and Saul returned to Antioch (Acts 12:25). They brought with them, a younger man, John Mark. The church in Antioch was blessed by the presence of prophets and teachers—inspired teachers who worked in helping the church mature. Acts 13:1 says: "Now in the church that was at Antioch there were certain prophets and teachers: Barnabas, Simeon who was called Niger, Lucius of Cyrene, Manaen who had been brought up with Herod the tetrarch, and Saul." Receiving instruction from the Holy Spirit, these men (along with the church cf. Acts 14:26-27) sent Barnabas, Saul, and John Mark out to preach. This begins what is commonly called "the first missionary journey of the Apostle Paul." Now the gospel is going "into all the world."

Other passages teach us that the roles of prophets and teachers were important to the first century church. Years later, Paul wrote to the Ephesians, saying, "And He Himself gave some to be apostles, some prophets, some evangelists, and some pastors and teachers, for the equipping of the saints for the work of ministry, for the edifying of the body of Christ" (Ephesians 4:11-12). Other churches had gifts, too (Romans 12:6; 1 Corinthians 12:10). The gift of prophecy was not relegated to Old Testament times (Acts 2:16-17).

"So, being sent out by the Holy Spirit, they went down to Seleucia, and from there they sailed to Cyprus" (Acts 13:4). Why Cyprus? Remember that this was Barnabas' home—a logical place to begin their preaching tour. After first stopping at the synagogue, they traveled the entire width of the island (ninety miles) to Paphos, the seat of the Roman government. There they met a sorcerer, Bar-Jesus, who was with the proconsul, Sergius Paulus. If, Sergius, as Luke says, was interested in hearing what these preachers had to say, why was he in the company of a sorcerer? It was common for officials to consult seers or sages for help in daily ministrations.

Saul (now called Paul for the first time) confronted Elymas. "O full of all deceit and all fraud, you son of the devil, you enemy of all righteousness, will you not cease perverting the straight ways of the Lord?" (Acts 13:10). The sorcerer was not a true son of Jesus (*Bar*-Jesus). If he was exposed as a fraud, his livelihood would be threatened. Now the tables are turned. Saul, struck blind on the Damascus Road, now strikes blind this child of the devil. God's judgment of darkness was fitting for one who opposed the light.

"Then the proconsul believed, when he saw what had been done, being astonished at the teaching of the Lord" (Acts 12:10). This man was shaken to the core at hearing and seeing the power of God. He believed. Luke uses "believe" several times in a comprehensive sense (Acts 14:1; 17:34; 19:18). This government official becomes a brand new Christian, a convert to Christ. There is no indication that he, as a Gentile, had any kind of association with Judaism (as might have been true of Cornelius).

Who knows what a church (congregation) might be able to do in sending out teachers of God's word. The Antioch church was a working church. Yes, they had inspired teachers. Today, we have the complete revelation of God—the New Testament of Jesus Christ. That message says "Go into all the world, preaching the gospel, to the Jew first and also to the Greek."

CHAPTER 63

Words of Wisdom

"And after the reading of the Law and the Prophets, the rulers of the synagogue sent to them, saying, "Men and brethren, if you have any word of exhortation for the people, say on."
(Acts 13:15)

Paul and Barnabas, after leaving the homeland of Barnabas, sailed northerly, arriving on the mainland of Asia Minor (often referred to as Galatia); their first brief stop was Perga. Paul was now drawing closer to his homeland. From Perga, John Mark went home, back to Jerusalem. Paul and others continued on to Antioch of Pisidia. This city (one of several Antiochs) was founded three hundred years before Paul's time by Seleucus I. Seleucus was one of several warriors/rulers who divided and sought control of the empire of Alexander the Great. Consequently, Antioch of Pisidia became a major center of Hellenism—the program that forced the Greek way of life on the inhabitants of a city or large land area. Because of Caesar Augustus, Antioch enjoyed Roman colony status. Interestingly, there were prominent women in this area who occupied civic offices; they later helped drive Paul out of the area (Acts 13:50).

According to custom, after reading (or, reciting) the *Shema* ("the Lord our God is one") and after "the reading of the Law and the Prophets," guests were invited to contribute to the teaching—teaching that came from the Old Testament. Jesus spoke of Himself from the Old Testament (Isaiah cf. Luke 4:16ff). Philip spoke of Jesus from the Old Testament (Acts 8:30-31). Now Paul is invited to teach from the Old Testament. Later in Acts Paul will preach to the Gentiles (Acts 9:15). Now, though, it is the Sabbath day and the audience is Jewish, comprised of "Men of Israel" (verses 16, 17, 23). Luke gives us Paul's sermon in capsule form. It is similar to, but shorter than, Stephen's sermon in Acts 7. The grand climax of both sermons was the coming of Jesus. "From this man's seed, according to the promise, God raised up for Israel a Savior, Jesus" (Acts 13:23). Jesus is not in the grave; He is alive (Acts 2:31). This was a theme of the Old Testament prophets these people read about during the synagogue services (Acts 3:18). Jesus is that prophet of whom Moses spoke (Acts 3:25). Paul picks up that same thread, briefly recounting the history of the Israelites. Beginning with the Egyptian bondage, moving into the wilderness, taking the land of Promise, the judges, and then the kings, Paul moves seamlessly through a familiar narrative.

Paul ties the story together by saying, "And when He had removed him, He raised up for them David as king, to whom also He gave testimony and said, 'I have found David the son of Jesse, a man after My own heart, who will do all My will'" (Acts 13:22). This is a point too great to be missed (Luke 1:32, 69; 2:4; Romans 1:3; 2 Timothy 2:8). John the Baptist came next; he was not the Christ, but he told people that Jesus of Nazareth was the Christ.

Why was Paul preaching? Why do we preach the gospel today? Why did Paul travel to lots of places in his work, carrying God's word? Why do we do the same today? It is because the people then and the people now—including you and me—need the gospel. So when Paul says, or some other preacher says, "Men and brethren, sons of the family of Abraham, and those among you who fear God, to you the word of this salvation has been sent," we need to listen.

CHAPTER 64

Barnabas, Paul, Zeus, Hermes

> "And Barnabas they called Zeus, and Paul, Hermes, because he was the chief speaker."
> (Acts 14:12)

The travels of Paul and Barnabas continued through the southeast region of Asia Minor. Iconium, a Greek city known for its agriculture and commerce, was their first stop. Their preaching brought a "violent attempt" (Acts 14:5) to drive them out of the city; they soon were on their way to Lystra and Derbe, located in the region of Lycaonia (Lycaonia, Phrygia, and Pisidia were the three regions of Galatia). "And they were preaching the gospel there" (Acts 14:7).

In an incident similar to that of Acts 3, Paul healed a lame man, crippled from birth. The miracle was instant—the man stood and walked. In amazement the citizens of Lystra cried out, "The gods have come down to us in the likeness of men!" (Acts 14:11). Barnabas and Paul were not men—they were the gods Zeus and Hermes (Greek names—Jupiter and Mercury are the Roman names)! Superstitious people believed that the gods sometimes visited their villages and cities. For example, the Roman poet Ovid, wrote in *Metamorphoses* about Zeus and Hermes visiting Phrygia. After being turned away by most of the citizens, the two gods found lodging with a peasant family. In the end, they destroyed the homes of those who had refused to show hospitality (*The Oxford Companion to Classical Civilization*, 509-510). Could that be why the citizens of Lystra began sacrificing to Paul and Barnabas—if they were gods, the people certainly did not want to offend them.

Paul did not speak from the Law of Moses. While this approach is found often in Acts (Acts 2:25-34; 7:2-47; 13:17-23), why would Paul use scripture these people had never heard or had any knowledge of? Paul said to worship the God of the universe rather than your lifeless, worthless idols. The God of heaven is the living God, the creator of all things. He is not arbitrary or capricious. He is patient, loving and desirous of the salvation of all. For a time, He allowed all men to walk in their own ways; still, He gave evidence for His own existence. The blessings of providence, rain, and sunshine testify to God's goodness. Importantly, the evidence that God gives imposes obligations on all. Paul made a similar point in Romans 1:20: "For since the creation of the world His invisible attributes are clearly seen, being understood by the things that are made, even His eternal power and Godhead, so that they are without excuse."

What was the result of the sermon? Luke says very little; it seems that Paul and Barnabas were able to stop the sacrifices (Acts 14:18). Then Jews from other places came and began opposing Paul. "They stoned Paul and dragged him out of the city, supposing him to be dead" (Acts 14:19). Then he got up and left with Barnabas for Derbe. Luke doesn't give us the details we wish we had. Later Paul said, "Three times I was beaten with rods; once I was stoned; three times I was shipwrecked; a night and a day I have been in the deep" (2 Corinthians 11:25). "From now on let no one trouble me, for I bear in my body the marks of the Lord Jesus" (Galatians 6:17). Paul was left for dead; but he was not dead. He was alive and continued to preach God's word.

The living God stood in stark contrast to the gods of Paul's time. Is it different today? What have you recognized as your god? Recognition from the world? Care, riches, and pleasures of life? Oh, we would never be idolaters! Really? Maybe we need to take a trip to Lystra with the Apostle Paul.

CHAPTER 65

Acts 15 and Bible Authority

Salvation in Christ was certainly "good news" for the Gentiles. "The Jews" first was the order of preaching beginning at Pentecost. Soon, those who were "aliens from the commonwealth of Israel and strangers from the covenants of promise" (Ephesians 2:12) were brought into the kingdom through the preaching of Peter (Acts 10, Cornelius) and Paul (Acts 13, Antioch of Pisidia). When Paul and others returned to Antioch of Syria, they spoke of their work among the Gentiles reporting "all that God had done with them, and that He had opened the door of faith to the Gentiles" (Acts 14:27).

The good reports did not mean that all was OK. In fact, a "doctrinal" issue, simmering at first, was getting hotter. While the Gentiles could be part of the kingdom, something the Jewish elders in Jerusalem admitted, the leaders were still quite concerned about the Gentiles being baptized but not being circumcised. Could a Gentile really be part of the kingdom when he retained his ethnic identity? Would the Gentiles have to make commitments to the Law of Moses in order to be accepted?

"And certain men came down from Judea and taught the brethren, 'Unless you are circumcised according to the custom of Moses, you cannot be saved'" (Acts 15:1). Whoever these men were, the fact that they came from Judea, the place where the gospel was first preached to the Jews, probably lent some credence to their objections regarding the Gentiles. After discussing the issue, Paul, Barnabas and others traveled to Jerusalem to visit the apostles and elders about the matter. Along the way they visited with other brethren telling about the reception of the Gentiles into Christ's church; this brought joy to all. Discussions in Jerusalem continued. Although God was working in the lives of the Gentiles (v. 4 "all things that God had done with them"), others objected. The Pharisees, in their zealousness, believed it was necessary "to circumcise them, and to command them to keep the law of Moses."

Peter's "sermon" (vv. 6-11) summarized his preaching to and the subsequent acceptance of the gospel by Cornelius and his household; he had spoken about these matters before (Acts 11). Peter concluded: Since God has accepted the Gentiles on the basis of faith, why can't you accept them in the same way? Why should you "test God by putting a yoke on the neck of the disciples which neither our fathers nor we were able to bear?" If the Jews could not gain salvation through obedience to the Law of Moses, why think the Gentiles could do so? Paul told the Galatians "that a man is not justified by the works of the law but by faith in Jesus Christ, even we have believed in Christ Jesus, that we might be justified by faith in Christ and not by the works of the law; for by the works of the law no flesh shall be justified I do not set aside the grace of God; for if righteousness comes through the law, then Christ died in vain" (Galatians 2:16-21).

God made no distinction between Jew and Gentile. All could be and can be saved by His grace, through faith in Christ. The gospel Paul and others preached was a "level playing field." The blessed gospel is for all. But that gospel is Christ's, not Paul's or Peter's or the Jews, or ours.

CHAPTER 66
Acts 15 and Bible Authority #2

After Peter finished speaking about his work with the household of Cornelius, Paul and Barnabas then gave their account (Acts 15:12). Paul was "a chosen vessel to bear the Lord's name before Gentiles." James spoke next (Acts 15:13-21). This James was evidently the brother of Jesus (Mark 6:3); he was with the disciples in Jerusalem after Jesus went back to heaven (Acts 1:14); and he saw Jesus alive after the Lord's resurrection (1 Corinthians 15:7). From other passages we can conclude that James had emerged as one of the leaders in the Jerusalem church. After his release from prison, Peter said to go and tell James what had happened (Acts 12:17). In Acts 15 James sums up what had happened to the Gentiles.

One of the interesting tacks James takes in recognizing the acceptance of the Gentiles is his appeal to the Old Testament—he quotes Amos 9:11-12. "'On that day I will raise up the tabernacle of David, which has fallen down, and repair its damages; I will raise up its ruins, And rebuild it as in the days of old; That they may possess the remnant of Edom, and all the Gentiles who are called by My name,' Says the LORD who does this thing." The dynasty of David was at an end; it lay in ruins. But one of the seed of David would arise and build the spiritual house of David. In this new house, the Messianic kingdom, Jews and Gentiles would be included ("the remnant of Edom"). James, the de facto leader of the circumcision, said the prophets would agree with what Peter and Paul had done.

James concludes, "Therefore I judge that we should not trouble those from among the Gentiles who are turning to God, but that we write to them to abstain from things polluted by idols, from sexual immorality, from things strangled, and from blood. For Moses has had throughout many generations those who preach him in every city, being read in the synagogues every Sabbath" (Acts 15:19-21). The need to abstain from idols, etc., predates the Law of Moses. While the Gentiles did not have to practice circumcision, it was needful that they respect the tender consciences of their newly found Jewish brethren. Scruples about eating meat used in idolatry was something Paul faced when working in Corinth (1 Corinthians 8-10).

The leaders sent out a letter (Acts 15:22-29) explaining their conclusions. It was clear that the leaders did not teach that the Gentiles had to be circumcised in order to be part of the kingdom. It was clear that the men they chose to deliver this letter were men approved of by all—approved and supported by the council, and third, their conclusions were not those of mere men—"For it seemed good to the Holy Spirit, and to us, to lay upon you no greater burden than these necessary things" (Acts 15:28). Paul, Barnabas, Judas, and Silas went back to Antioch; they delivered the letter; the brethren were encouraged.

Disagreements among God's people are not new. Discussions, even heated at times, are necessary to learn, grapple with, and come to a better understanding of any given Bible issue. Attitudes that make for peace are needed by all. Animosities can arise, especially in the heat of spiritual battle. Yet, if God's people will always have the attitude of wanting to know what God says—God, not man—then they are well-served and well-positioned to come to the truth of the matter. Implicit in Acts 15 are the different ways God teaches us in His word. Acts 15 is all about Bible authority.

CHAPTER 67

Acts 15 and Bible Authority #3

"For it seemed good to the Holy Spirit, and to us, to lay upon you no greater burden than these necessary things."
(Acts 15:28)

When the leaders of the Jerusalem church along with Paul, Barnabas and others, discussed the matter of whether the Gentiles needed to adhere to certain aspects of the Law of Moses, their conclusion was predicated on what the Holy Spirit said. That is, they did not arbitrarily decide that the Gentiles did not have to be circumcised; rather, they had communication (direct) from God, the Holy Spirit (Acts 5:4). To put it another way, they were respecting the express authority of God. Bible believers still cling to that great principle. Colossians 3:17 says, "And whatever you do in word or deed, do all in the name of the Lord Jesus, giving thanks to God the Father through Him."

A good question to ask is: How does the Bible teach us? How does God express His will? Some common examples will help us better understand exactly how God teaches us in His word. Jesus, in giving His great commission, said that He had all authority (Matthew 28:18-20). Therefore, when the apostles were going into all the world, the message they preached was the message invested with Christ's authority; it was not their message; it was Christ's. "Whatever you bind on earth shall have been bound in heaven; and whatever you loose on earth shall have been loosed in heaven" (NASV Matthew 18:18). The Lord's will has already been decided—by Him! That will was (is) lived out in the lives of those who are faithfully serving the Lord (Philippians 4:9). How Christ's authority is expressed can be seen in His instructions about the Lord's Supper. Luke 22:19 says: "And He took bread, gave thanks and broke it, and gave it to them, saying, 'This is my body which is given for you; do this in remembrance of Me.'" This is a direct command or statement from the Lord. Later we find New Testament Christians remembering what the Lord said; they then, in obedience, followed His will (1 Corinthians 11:23-24). This leads us to the example of New Testament Christians as they lived out the Lord's will. Paul said, "Imitate me, just as I also imitate Christ" (1 Corinthians 11:1). That is, when I do the will of Christ, follow my example. And we have an example of New Testament Christians partaking of the Lord's Supper; in fact, this example tells us when they observed the memorial feast. "Now on the first day of the week, when the disciples came together to break bread, Paul, ready to depart the next day, spoke to them and continued his message until midnight" (Acts 20:7). We ask: Did these New Testament Christians partake of the Supper once a year or once a month, or every first day of the week? It is necessarily inferred (necessary inference, an inference that *must be* inferred) that these early Christians took the Lord's Supper every first day of the week. If you don't believe that, then on what first day of the week did they observe the Supper? The Jews, under the Law of Moses, observed the Sabbath Day, keeping it holy. Which Sabbath day? Did they observe the Sabbath once a year or once a month? As often as a Sabbath day rolled around they were obligated to observe that day in service to God. As often as a first day of the week rolls around, we are obligated to observe the Lord's Supper.

Some today laugh at and scorn the words written above. That is, some hold in contempt the teaching that direct command, approved apostolic example, and necessary inference have anything to do in expressing God's will. If you believe that, then tell us HOW the word of God teaches and authorizes?

CHAPTER 68

Acts 15 and Bible Authority #4

Did the Gentiles have to be circumcised in order to be part of the kingdom? The experiences and preaching of Peter and Paul said no. James, a leader in the Jerusalem church appealed to Old Testament prophecy (Amos 9:11-12) and said no. How was God expressing His will about this live issue that confronted these New Testament Christians? Were they left alone, without any teaching or guidance from the Lord? Would they just decide for themselves what they should do? Would they just do what was best as long as they were sincere in their motivation?

Direct command, approved apostolic example, and necessary inference are at least three ways by which the Lord teaches us His will. Read the following from Brother Doy Moyer, gospel preacher, who lives in Birmingham, Alabama.

"Regardless of who it is interpreting Scripture, there is a basic process, often unspoken, employed by anyone who thinks Scripture is authoritative that cannot be denied without denying fundamental logic or sounding outright silly. This process involves looking directly at what is said, considering examples given, and then inferring from what is said and shown how important and applicable these matters are. Even those who fuss and pejoratively poke at CENI (Command, Example, Necessary Inference) do the same. At the end of the day, if they are going to say, 'this is what Christians ought to believe or do,' they will only get there through the same means. They will appeal to what Scripture says, to the examples provided, and through a reasoning process (inferring) come to conclusions that they think are important. So it is with everyone. Everyone! People will differ on outcomes, but there is no denying the process of how communication works. It astounds me when some try to deny it" (accessed from *Mind Your Faith* website www.vestaviachurchofchrist.com).

Brother Moyer is writing about critics who want to reject the DC, AE, and NI model in establishing Bible teaching. At the end of the day, however, these same critics of "tradition" or "back water thinking" employ the same methods in their own study of the Bible.

It is not just the Bible in which these methods are employed. We use the same kind of logic and understanding in everyday walks of life. Suppose you go to the meat counter at Walmart and ask for one pound of "Black Forest ham." The worker behind the counter understands immediately what you want—you want one pound of Black Forest ham. Do you want thin sliced or thick sliced? You answer: Thin sliced. Why do we understand what's happening here? It is because words mean something. Ham means ham, not turkey. Thin means thin, not thick. One pound means one pound, not two pounds. Also, you don't have to say, "I don't want any cheese." The clerk understands that you asked for ham, not cheese. The necessary inference is that you want what you asked for and nothing else. You did not authorize the clerk to give you cheese.

To be sure, getting at what the Bible is saying is more important than buying something at Walmart. But the same principles of learning and logic and understanding apply in these various realms of life. God told Noah to build an ark out of gopher wood. God didn't say, "Now, Noah, don't use pine or cedar." Why? It is because the command to use gopher wood excluded the use of all other woods. Partaking of the Lord's Supper on the Lord's Day, the first day of the week, follows the example of New Testament Christians. The day is specified; the time of day is not. We all need to study the Bible more than we do. And we need to constantly, carefully examine what God wants us to believe and then do. Anything less disrespects the authority of our Lord.

CHAPTER 69

Acts 15 and Bible Authority #5

The question we should always ask when thinking about what to do in our service to the Lord is this: What does the Lord authorize? What does His will say about what we want to do or what we think we need to do? Do we have some kind of teaching from the Lord about any given matter? Let's return to three common ways the Bible teaches us—direct command, approved apostolic example, and necessary inference. How does Acts 15 help us understand and apply these principles from God's word? Or, can we even find these principles in Acts 15 (or, elsewhere in the Bible)?

Peter's speech (Acts 15:7-11) recounts his work with Cornelius, the first Gentile convert (Acts 10). His words are predicated on what happened in Acts 10 and 11; from this a necessary conclusion can be drawn. In Acts 10 Peter saw in a vision animals of all kinds coming down from heaven. When he was told to arise and kill and eat, he said, "Not so, Lord! For I have never eaten anything common or unclean. And a voice spoke to him again the second time, what God has cleansed you must not call common" (Acts 10:14-15). Peter got the point. He said, "In truth I perceive that God shows no partiality" (Acts 10:34). At the conclusion of his sermon he asked: "Can anyone forbid water, that these should not be baptized who have received the Holy Spirit just as we have?" (Acts 10:47). Of course, no one could forbid baptism for Cornelius.

The speech Paul and Barnabas made in Acts 15:12 illustrates the validity of approved apostolic examples. Their work (Acts 13 and 14) involved preaching to the uncircumcised; God approved of what they did by the miracles they worked (Acts 13:11-12). Acts 14:27 says, "Now when they had come and gathered the church together, they reported all that God had done with them, and that He had opened the door of faith to the Gentiles." GOD was working among the Gentiles; GOD approved the actions of Paul and Barnabas; GOD said the Gentiles could be saved by the gospel, without circumcision. Acts 15:12 is a summary of what Paul and Barnabas had done in their work among the Gentiles.

James, in Acts 15:13-21, provides a direct statement from scripture. The scripture is Amos 9:11-12. James mentions what Peter had said and done. James then says: "And with this the words of the prophets agree, just as it is written." That is, the Old Testament prophets in anticipated the inclusion of the Gentiles into the family of God; they and Peter were in agreement. "It is written." This is what God expressly said. Paul, Barnabas, Peter, and James all recognized that God wanted the Gentiles to hear and obey the gospel.

In fairness, we would admit that Acts 15 does not resolve all of the questions that might be asked about Bible authority. But a larger consideration remains. It is this: When we are trying to find out what God wants us to do in our service to Him, how do we go about that task? Do we just jettison God's word and say it doesn't matter? Or, do we do the hard work of studying—with good and honest and open hearts—what the Bible says, as we seek answers to the questions that are very real and important to us as Christians? If our constant desire is to know what God says, then we are on the right track. Anything less than a desire to seek God's counsel disrespects His authority.

CHAPTER 70

The Church at Philippi

When Paul and Silas left Antioch, embarking on what is commonly styled "Paul's second missionary journey," these preachers were continuing the work that began in Jerusalem in Acts 2 on the Day of Pentecost. The Lord said, "You shall be witnesses to Me in Jerusalem, and in all Judea and Samaria, and to the end of the earth" (Acts 1:8). The pattern continues, as now Paul and others make their way for the first time onto what we might call European soil. Answering the Macedonian call meant that Paul would begin traversing the great cities of Macedonia and Achaia. In doing so the Apostle would establish relationships with churches—Christians—that meant much to him in subsequent years. Leaving Troas, located on the extreme northwest tip of Asia Minor, the travelers crossed the Aegean Sea and soon arrived at Philippi. Evidently, Paul linked up with Luke at Troas. Acts 16:10 uses the pronoun "we" indicating that Luke was now part of this preaching effort.

Acts 16:12 says, "And from there to Philippi, which is the foremost city of that part of Macedonia, a colony. And we were staying in that city for some days." Philippi is so named after Philip of Macedon (father of Alexander the Great) and eventually became a Roman colony. Its population included many soldiers who, in exchange for service to Caesar, were given land and opportunities in this choice area of northeast Macedonia. Roman colonies enjoyed the benefits of the crown—favorable taxes, good roads, military protection, and business connections. Located on a main thoroughfare, Philippi was situated to do well in most every aspect of first century life. As a Roman colony the city also recognized its allegiance to the Emperor cult. And why not worship the emperor? After all, he was the "god" that made all good things possible!

In this context Paul and others began their work of preaching. First, they met a godly woman, Lydia, a business woman, who sold expensive purple dye (purple was the color of royalty). She was a woman of some means; she had a household and had the ability to show hospitality to these traveling preachers. Lydia was a worshiper of God; she and other women had gathered by the riverbank for prayer. She heard the gospel; in doing so, the Lord opened her heart; she listened to the message Paul preached; she obeyed God's word. However, not only did Lydia hear and believe and obey the gospel; her household did the same. But no one in this conversion account obeyed the Lord before hearing and believing the gospel message. If there were people incapable of hearing and understanding the gospel (not accountable), then certainly Paul did not baptize them. If you are going to prove that "infant baptism" took place in Acts 16, the following would need to be true. Was Lydia a married woman with children? Were these children with her in Philippi? Were some of these children infants? Were these infant children baptized? Prove these necessary things and you might have a case for infant baptism. Anything short of absolute proof will not do. Did she have a husband? Luke does not mention it. Lydia said "Come to my house." Later (Acts 16:40) when Paul and Silas got out of prison, they went to *Lydia's house*. Bible baptism is for people who can hear, understand, and act upon the message of the Lord. Bible baptism is for those who are lost in sin; they understand their alienation from God because of their sin; they know they need to repent; they have sins from which to repent. None of this is true of babies.

Acts 16:14 says, "The Lord opened her heart to heed the things spoken by Paul." If her heart was opened, then wasn't her heart at some time closed? Why would a heart be closed? If Lydia was a proselyte, then misconceptions about the nature of the kingdom might be part of the picture. Christ was a stumbling block to many (1 Corinthians 1:23). Notice that Lydia "heard us." Then the Lord opened her heart. Is your heart closed? Have you heard the word of God and have yet to act upon that message? The Lord will do for you exactly what He did for Lydia. The question is: Do you want Him to?

CHAPTER 71

Thessalonica: A World Turned Upside Down

Carrying the wounds and insults of Philippi, Paul and his fellow travelers made their way 90 miles west southwest along the Via Egnatia, and soon arrived in Thessalonica. "Now when they had passed through Amphipolis and Apollonia, they came to Thessalonica, where was a synagogue of the Jews" (Acts 17:1). Later, when writing to the Thessalonians, Paul spoke of his time in Philippi. "Having suffered before and been shamefully treated, as ye know, at Philippi, we waxed bold in our God to speak unto you the gospel of God in much conflict" (1 Thessalonians 2:2). The Apostle to the Gentiles was not deterred in his pursuit of the gospel.

Thessalonica was founded by Cassander, king of Macedonia in 315 BC. Its strategic location on the Aegean Sea produced a lively economy. Its status as a "free city" in Roman times meant that the citizens of Thessalonica had some leeway in their own government. Acts 17:6 speaks of the "rulers of the city." Thessalonica was the largest city of Macedonia; we are not surprised to read about Paul immediately going into the synagogue—the obvious meeting place for Jews. What did Paul say?

"It behooved the Christ to suffer, and to rise again from the dead; and that this Jesus, whom, said he, I proclaim unto you, is the Christ" (Acts 17:3). Paul's message was the same as that of Jesus, when the Savior spoke to the Jews during His ministry. "The Son of man must suffer many things, and be rejected of the elders and chief priests and scribes and be killed, and the third day be raised up" (Luke 9:22). The message of the crucified and risen Savior is the constant message throughout the book of Acts. Too, the story of Jesus of Nazareth was integral to Paul's message. This was often a sticking point in accepting or rejecting the gospel. The Jews did not deny that a Messiah would come; they did not, though, believe that Jesus of Nazareth was that Messiah. The capstone of Paul's teaching was: "this Jesus…is the Christ." Paul explained and demonstrated and reasoned from the Scriptures. His conclusion is: This is that. Jesus is the fulfillment of what you have been reading about in your synagogue services. Paul placed one thing along side of another—the historical Jesus is essential to a true message of the gospel. Jesus is not a myth; He is not mystical; He was/is real, alive and well. That is what the message of the gospel is all about. What reaction did Paul's preaching produce? "Some were persuaded" and "some were not persuaded" (Acts 17:4-5). Devout Greeks—God-fearers, including several women—accepted the message. Acts 20:4 mentions two men from Thessalonica: Aristarchus and Secundus. Envious Jews, however, stirred up opposition to Paul's work.

"These that have turned the world upside down are come hither also" (Acts 17:6). Paul and his fellow-workers were accused of fomenting political strife. They were "acting contrary to the decrees of Caesar." The Jews played their oft-used trump card: These men have another king. This was a serious charge; the consequences could be fatal. Yet, Paul was not a political or social radical. He was a preacher who sought to turn the hearts of people everywhere to the Lord. Their lives and ours will be turned upside down when, but only when, we yield to Jesus, the Christ, the Messiah. King Jesus must always come first.

CHAPTER 72

Corinth: The Church of God

"After these things Paul departed from Athens and went to Corinth."
(Acts 18:1)

Paul's work in Athens was not entirely profitable; still, some were favorably inclined to his message about the Unknown God. The notion of a final judgment and resurrection from the dead caused some to mock; others wanted to hear more. Paul's work in larger, urban cities of the first century is interesting. It has only been in the last two hundred years or so that the world has been populated with cities of over one million citizens; rural cultures have given way to large metropolitan centers of influence. Corinth was one of the larger cities in New Testament times; its first century population is hard to determine; 200,000 would be a good guess. Volumes have been written about Corinth. Its history, influence, commercial appeal, and debauchery provide clues as to its prominence. The hosting of the Isthmian Games every two years made Corinth a center of attraction.

Paul had been hounded out of city after city. Still, he continued his quest for souls. We are not surprised to find him reasoning "in the synagogue every Sabbath" and persuading "both Jews and Greeks" (Acts 18:4). Paul met a couple, Aquila and Priscilla, Jews who had recently left Rome. The association of these three Christians now becomes a frequent aspect of Luke's history. Paul was glad when Timothy and Silas arrived from Macedonia; they had stayed behind to work with the Christians in Thessalonica (1 Thessalonians 3:2). Paul's preaching produced some good results.

Paul challenged the intellectual climate of Corinth with his message about Jesus. Later, he wrote to the Corinthians saying: "And I, brethren, when I came to you, did not come with excellence of speech or of wisdom declaring to you the testimony of God. For I determined not to know anything among you except Jesus Christ and Him crucified" (1 Corinthians 2:1-2). The collective wisdom of the ages, the sage teachings of Greek philosophers, and the supposed ability of "man" to know more than God, stood in stark contrast to the "foolishness of God." Yet, it is this message that fell into good and honest hearts.

"Then Crispus, the ruler of the synagogue, believed on the Lord with all his household. And many of the Corinthians, hearing, believed and were baptized" (Acts 18:8). First in the synagogue and then in private homes, Paul spread the word. Crispus, a Jew, along with his household (those who could understand and needed to respond to the gospel) "believed." That is, they accepted by faith the gospel of Christ and obeyed the Savior. "Many Corinthians" did the same. This surely would have included Gentiles.

First Corinthians begins this way: "Paul, called to be an apostle of Jesus Christ through the will of God, and Sosthenes our brother, To the church of God which is at Corinth, to those who are sanctified in Christ Jesus, called to be saints, with all who in every place call on the name of Jesus Christ our Lord, both theirs and ours" (1:1-2). What is the church of God? It is people who hear, believe, and obey God's word. What is the church of Christ? It is people who hear, believe, and obey God's word. The Lord told Paul to be bold in preaching; there were many in Corinth who would accept the message of salvation. He continued working for eighteen months. If Paul did what he did in Corinth, could the same thing be done in the city where you live?

CHAPTER 73

Ephesus: The City of Diana

> "And it came to pass, that, while Apollos was at Corinth, Paul having passed through the upper coasts came to Ephesus: and finding certain disciples."
> (Acts 19:1)

Upon arriving, Paul found "certain disciples," indicating that the gospel had already made some progress in Ephesus. True, these new acquaintances needed more teaching about the baptism of John the Baptist and baptism by the authority of Christ; still, their acceptance of newfound truth as preached by Paul indicates that they had "good and honest" hearts. Soon, true to form, Paul began working in the synagogue, reasoning and persuading all who would listen about God and His kingdom (Acts 19:8). The stage is set for an eventful three years of preaching. Paul was busy. Acts 19:10 says, "And this continued by the space of two years; so that all they which dwelt in Asia heard the word of the Lord Jesus, both Jews and Greeks."

Settlement of western Asia or Asia Minor dates to 133 BC when the kingdom of Pergamum was strong. This area (true of most) passed through Medo-Persian hands before falling under the sway of Greek influence. In time, the Romans dominated. Ephesus was allowed some leeway in self-government; Asiarchs, local officials, were able to "rule" the city, but under the watchful eye of the mother city, Rome (Acts 19:31).

Diana (Roman name) or Artemis (Greek name) prevailed over the city of Ephesus. "And when the town clerk had appeased the people, he said, Ye men of Ephesus, what man is there that knoweth not how that the city of the Ephesians is a worshipper of the great goddess Diana, and of the image which fell down from Jupiter?" (Acts 19:35). The temple of Diana, larger than the Parthenon in Athens, became one of the "seven wonders of the world." Diana's influence was such that "all Asia and the world" worshiped her (Acts 19:27). A thriving "cottage industry" revolved around silversmiths and their handiwork (Acts 19:24). Obviously, anything that might upset the "status quo," especially when it involved money would be suspect.

The gospel challenges anything—money, idols, self—that tries to take the place of the living God. Paul's preaching was accompanied by miracles. This resulted in many coming to the Lord. True repentance of idolatry is indicated by the fact that these people "burned" their books of magic; a stupendous sum of 50,000 pieces of silver—50,000 days wages! The result? "So the word of the Lord grew mightily and prevailed" (Acts 19:20). A riot soon ensued. The charge was mostly accurate. "This Paul has persuaded and turned away many people, saying that they are not gods which are made with hands" (Acts 19:26). That was the message of Paul to the idolaters of Athens. Paul wrote to the Corinthians saying, "If, in the manner of men, I have fought with beasts at Ephesus" (1 Corinthians 15:32). Whether real or metaphorical, the beasts were a danger to Paul.

Today, Ephesus lies in ruins. Hardly a trace of its former glory can be seen. But what about people of "the Way" (Acts 19:9)? Are these folks still around? Are there still, today, people who leave idols behind in order to know the true, living God of the universe? Are there still today people with honesty of heart, who, after hearing and seeing the power of God, will make active changes in their lives? If the gospel remains the power of God unto salvation, then, today, as in first century Ephesus, there must be some of those people somewhere. Are you one of them?

CHAPTER 74

Acts 20: Upon the First Day of the Week

Paul's long-held desire was to visit Rome (Acts 19:21). From this point forward in Luke's narrative, the Apostle's inexorable march to the center of the world dominates. Much of Paul's work during this time involved the collection for the poor saints in Jerusalem; he wrote about this to the Corinthians and the Romans. Leaving Ephesus, Paul visited churches in Macedonia and Greece; surely the churches in Philippi, Berea, and Thessalonica were glad to see their beloved teacher. Was it during this time that Corinth experienced a "painful visit" from Paul? (2 Corinthians 2:1). Then traveling across the Aegean Sea to Troas, Paul met friends—brethren well-attested to by frequent references in the New Testament (Ephesians 6; Colossians 4; 2 Timothy 4).

"Now on the first day of the week, when the disciples came together to break bread, Paul, ready to depart the next day, spoke to them and continued his message until midnight" (Acts 20:7). F. F. Bruce made this comment about Acts 20:7 (quoted in Stott, *Acts*, 319): "Luke's reference to the 'first day of the week,' i.e., Sunday, 'is the earliest unambiguous evidence we have for the Christian practice of gathering together to worship on that day.'" Today, as New Testament Christians, we can hardly afford to overlook this significant passage. It has become a battle ground for arguments, discussions, and even divisions among God's people. It is doubtful, though, that Luke intended such. The "we" in (Acts 20:6) tells us that Luke was there; he provides a firsthand, eyewitness account. What can we learn from this passage about how we today, should worship God?

First, clearly, these Christians assembled to partake of the Lord's Supper. Some waited for Paul to arrive; after five days he was present with them; "we" stayed seven days. The chronology suggests that they were deliberate about waiting and being together on the Lord's Day that they might partake of the Supper. Next, Paul preached. We joke about how long he preached. How long depends on when he started and whether this was this Roman time or Jewish time. Whatever the time was, it was "dark." Surely, Paul's message was consistent with other preaching that he did; this time, though, in the company of Christians, he may have sought to encourage them, exhort them, and bless them with God's word. At the end of the gathering, all ate together (Acts 20:11). This was a common meal of some kind in contrast to the Lord's Supper, which is not a common meal (1 Corinthians 11). Another lesson emerges from Acts 20:7, a passage often used in discussions about Bible authority.

How often do we partake of the Supper? The "religious world" is hopelessly divided about the matter. If these New Testament Christians partook of the Supper on the first day of the week, and they did, should we do the same? Should we partake of the Supper every time there is a first day of the week? If not, then who will decide which first day of the week the Supper should be observed? Clearly, Paul and others came together to break bread. And from the travel and waiting and coming together it seems clear that they wanted to be together on the Lord's Day to partake of the Supper, and not on some other day. When did the Jews observe the Sabbath? You answer: Each time there was a Sabbath. If Sabbath means every Sabbath, would not the "first day of the week" mean every first day of the week?

Implied in this account is the fact that Bible authority can be established by *approved apostolic example*. Think about it: IF Acts 20:7 does not bind every first day of the week observance of the Lord's Supper, then you and I don't have clear instructions from the Lord as to when we should remember His death on the cross for our sins. What say you?

CHAPTER 75

Acts 21: I Am Ready to Die

"Then Paul answered, 'What do you mean by weeping and breaking my heart? For I am ready not only to be bound, but also to die at Jerusalem for the name of the Lord Jesus.'"
(Acts 21:13)

Tears and embraces were the memories Paul cherished as he said goodbye, probably for the last time, to the elders of the church in Ephesus. Paul's two main concerns during this time were that he wanted to visit Rome and needed to return to Jerusalem to deliver benevolent aid contributed by the churches of Achaia and Macedonia for the poor saints in Jerusalem. So, he begins his final trip to the City of David. Even though the prophet Agabus warned about impending danger, Paul would not be deterred. Luke says, "And after those days we packed and went up to Jerusalem" (Acts 21:15).

After arriving in Jerusalem, Paul immediately visited with James and the elders of the church. Inclusion of the Gentiles into the kingdom remained a matter of interest for these men; Paul's work continued to be consistent with the discussions that took place in Acts 15. The fact that James and others appealed to Paul to help four Jewish men complete their vows shows that they (Jews) had not given up all attachments to the Law of Moses. Too, others were watching Paul. Did the Apostle really tell Jews to repudiate the Law of Moses and circumcision and certain customs? Certainly, Paul was favorably inclined toward the Jews; his concern partially explains the collection for the poor in the city; this aid would help solidify Jewish-Gentile relations. Luke's brief comment about the aid leaves us wondering about the collection, who got what, what did they say when Paul delivered the funds, etc. "And when we had come to Jerusalem, the brethren received us gladly" (Acts 21:17; Romans 15:31). The charges against Paul were false; his actions with the four men show that the charges were false. Some believe Paul did wrong; do you? Paul was willing to give an accommodation to the Jews as long as it did not violate the gospel doctrine of salvation by grace through faith in Jesus, apart from the works of the Law of Moses. 1 Corinthians 9:19-22 explains his actions: "For though I am free from all men, I have made myself a servant to all, that I might win the more; and to the Jews I became as a Jew, that I might win Jews; to those who are under the law, as under the law, that I might win those who are under the law; to those who are without law, as without law (not being without law toward God, but under law toward Christ), that I might win those who are without law; to the weak I became as weak, that I might win the weak. I have become all things to all men, that I might by all means save some." When a concession could be made, even to Judaism, Paul was willing to make it as long as the gospel was not altered. In Galatians 2, Paul was unwilling to circumcise Titus because the Judaizers insisted on it being done.

These events attracted attention. Paul was soon taken into custody by Jews from Asia. Only the arrival of Roman soldiers prevented his immediate death; he was taken into custody by the soldiers and centurions; at this point the Jews knew they had to desist in trying to kill Paul. As in Corinth, Paul was now rescued from his own countrymen (2 Corinthians 11:26) by a Roman soldier. Violent rage and religious prejudice threw Paul into a Roman jail. For a time, he was safe. But surely remembered his words to friends: "For I am ready not only to be bound, but also to die at Jerusalem for the name of the Lord Jesus."

CHAPTER 76

Acts 22: I Am a Jew, Born in Tarsus

Paul's detractors assumed that he had brought a Gentile into the temple; they were wrong. The chief captain, Claudius Lysias, was wrong to assume that Paul was the notorious Egyptian assassin. Paul said, "I am indeed a Jew, born in Tarsus of Cilicia, but brought up in this city at the feet of Gamaliel, taught according to the strictness of our fathers' law, and was zealous toward God as you all are today" (Acts 22:3). With these words he began the first of several defenses before those gathered in Jerusalem. His *apologia* was a masterpiece of sensitivity and accommodation and elucidation to his Jewish audience. The charge of Acts 21:28, "This is the man who teaches all men everywhere against the people, the law, and this place; and furthermore he also brought Greeks into the temple and has defiled this holy place" was serious; if true, then Paul's life was in jeopardy. Knowing the charges were false, Paul took pains to make it clear that he still had great attachment to his Jewish heritage and faith. This was not in any way a compromise of the gospel of Christ.

Paul spoke to his audience in Hebrew/Aramaic; this would have quieted the crowd. His upbringing placed him in the middle of Jewish learning. Acts 5:34 says, "Then one in the council stood up, a Pharisee named Gamaliel, a teacher of the law held in respect by all the people, and commanded them to put the apostles outside for a little while." Paul's association with this noted teacher was in his favor. No one could doubt his Jewishness; he was a Hebrew of the Hebrews (Philippians 3:5). His zeal matched that of his enemies; he had been zealous in his pursuit of those of the Way. Surely the Sanhedrin would have known this to be true. Moving from personal asides to his Damascus Road experience, Paul spoke his encounter with the very one whom he had been persecuting, namely, Jesus Christ. Arriving in Damascus, Paul met Ananias—a man recognized by all to have a good reputation. With his sight restored, Paul was "chosen" that he "should know His will, and see the Just One, and hear the voice of His mouth" (Acts 22:14). Paul became the apostle to the Gentiles. Acts 22:16 says, "And now why are you waiting? Arise and be baptized, and wash away your sins, calling on the name of the Lord." Paul, now in Christ, began to preach about Christ.

How did the crowd react? "And they listened to him until this word, and then they raised their voices and said, 'Away with such a fellow from the earth, for he is not fit to live!' Then, as they cried out and tore off their clothes and threw dust into the air" (Acts 22:22-23). Gentiles could become proselytes; but they could not become proselytes without first becoming Jews via circumcision and adherence to at least parts of the Law of Moses. Jews were superior to Gentiles; the gospel said otherwise. All are one in Christ and stand on equal spiritual ground.

The truth of Paul's message was that he remained in continuity with the God of his fathers. That God, the God of the Old Testament, told the Jews through the mouths of the prophets that Messiah would come and die for all. How could Paul preach anything less than that? Inclusion of the Gentiles into the kingdom was a matter of prophecy. Sometimes, though, prejudice keeps people from even considering the truth of God. The consequences of such rejection can be fatal. This time Paul's life was in danger; and the souls of men and women were in danger, too.

CHAPTER 77

Acts 23: Hope and Resurrection of the Dead

Claudius Lysias wanted to find the truth about the charges against Paul. Intending at first to "beat the truth out of Paul," the Apostle's Roman citizenship prevented that extreme measure. So the commander made an appeal to the chief priests and Sanhedrin, led by the unsavory Ananias. The priests and especially the high priest controlled the temple; consequently, they controlled the money. Ananias was well-known for withholding money that should have gone to the temple priests. The words "Sanhedrin" or "council" or "meeting" date to the period between the testaments and the rule of the Hasmoneans. First Maccabees speaks of Jonathan the high priest, the elders of nation, and the priests (1 Maccabees 12:6). References in the New Testament (Matthew 16:21; Mark 8:31; 11:27; 14:43; Luke 9:22) acted as a kind of appellate court (a court of review of lower court decisions). Typically, the number of members of the Sanhedrin is set at 70; that number, though, has been disputed (Ferguson, *Backgrounds of Early Christianity*, 533-536).

Paul's appeal to a good conscience brought a slap on the mouth from Ananias; why this abrupt beginning? Smiting someone on the mouth would be easier than disproving such a statement. And we can only wonder as to why Paul did not know Ananias was the high priest at that time. Paul was aware that acting in such a manner was contrary to the Law; surely he did not deliberately so act. Seeing a divided crowd, Pharisees and Sadducees, Paul "cried out in the council, 'Men and brethren, I am a Pharisee, the son of a Pharisee; concerning the hope and resurrection of the dead I am being judged!'" (Acts 23:6). This declaration created immediate dissension in the assembly. Paul as a Pharisee shared with others the great hope of the resurrection. Jesus silenced the Sadducees (Luke 20:27ff) when He taught that God is the God of the living and that all will one day be raised. In the end, the Pharisees took up for Paul.

The crowd was nearly out of control; the commander took Paul back to the safety of his jail cell. He was not alone. "The following night the Lord stood by him and said, 'Be of good cheer, Paul; for as you have testified for Me in Jerusalem, so you must also bear witness at Rome,'" (Acts 23:11). Now Paul knew that he would live; he would endure several more trials; still, he would finally travel to Rome fulfilling his long-held desire to visit his brethren in the royal city. How could Paul not believe in the resurrection? He had seen the risen Savior on the Damascus Road. Paul's persecutions were real; surely he did not enjoy tribulations, distresses, stripes, imprisonments, tumults, and sleeplessness (2 Corinthians 6:4-5). Now, though, the Lord stands by him, encouraging and strengthening him. Paul's life would not come to an end in Jerusalem. The Lord, not the Apostle, was in charge of his circumstances. Paul endured much before finally getting to Rome. But when he got there, the Lord was still with him.

CHAPTER 78

The Convenient Season

"And after some days, when Felix came with his wife Drusilla, who was Jewish, he sent for Paul and heard him concerning the faith in Christ. Now as he reasoned about righteousness, self-control, and the judgment to come, Felix was afraid and answered, 'Go away for now; when I have a convenient time I will call for you.'"
(Acts 24:24-25)

When Paul stood before Felix, the Apostle stood in the midst of power—Roman power. The geographical dominion of Rome stretched "from sea to shining sea." If it was true (it was not) that Paul was really a seditious fellow, that charge could easily be leveled anywhere in the empire. Too, the religious tentacles of Jerusalem wrapped around most places Paul traveled. While Rome and Jerusalem were natural enemies, they would easily unite in getting rid of someone or anyone who upset the status quo, whether religious or political. Now Paul is on trial. Luke tells us, "When he had come, the Jews who had come down from Jerusalem stood about and laid many serious complaints against Paul, which they could not prove, while he answered for himself, 'Neither against the law of the Jews, nor against the temple, nor against Caesar have I offended in anything at all,'" (Acts 25:7-8). In five different trials Paul stood before the Jews (Acts 21:40), before the Sanhedrin (Acts 23:1), before Felix (Acts 24:1), before Festus (Acts 25:1), and before King Agrippa II (Acts 25:23). In each instance, the charge of sedition or sacrilege could not be proven.

Tertullus, a lawyer, charged Paul with three crimes. First, he said Paul was a troublemaker. Second, Paul was a ringleader of the sect of the

Nazarenes. Third, Paul had tried to desecrate the temple. Perhaps in an appeal to Felix's vanity, Tertullus told the governor that he (Felix) could easily see these charges were true when he personally examined Paul. Paul answered the charges one by one. What would Felix do? Paul was innocent (Acts 23:9, 29); but Felix, hoping for a bribe, (Acts 24:26) kept Paul in jail. However, when Felix called for Paul again, in order to hear things "concerning the faith in Christ," the governor got much more than he bargained for.

Drusilla was the youngest daughter of Herod Agrippa I (Acts 12); she was the sister of Bernice and Herod Agrippa II. History speaks of her great beauty. At this time, she was the third wife of Felix. Felix was known for unusual cruelty and fits of temper. With this brief background, we can better understand Paul's sermon to this couple. Words of righteousness, self-control, and judgment were applied to this couple. People of iniquity are unrighteous; they need to know how they can stand right before God. People who live with no self-control—in this case, as Felix seduced Drusilla away from her husband—need the restraints of God's word. All people need to be warned about the judgment to come. Intemperate people, people who live to satisfy their own lusts, need to know that judgment is coming.

Felix was terrified upon hearing Paul. Did waves of guilt wash across his soul? Was his conscience awakened, if only for a moment? Did the convenient season ever come for Felix? Typically, we say no; and there is no record of his conversion to Jesus. "Meanwhile he also hoped that money would be given him by Paul, that he might release him. Therefore he sent for him more often and conversed with him" (Acts 24:26). Is it ever convenient to give up power, money, and lust? Felix didn't think so. What say you?

CHAPTER 79

Paul Before Festus

"Now when Festus had come to the province, after three days he went up from Caesarea to Jerusalem."
(Acts 25:1)

After taking over the reins of leadership from Felix, Festus quickly became acquainted with the myriads of political and religious issues in Palestine. One case was that of Paul. The Apostle had lingered in prison for two years because of Felix's ulterior motives. Now Paul would begin again, before a new governor, to answer the false charges of the Jews. "Then the high priest and the chief men of the Jews informed him against Paul; and they petitioned him, asking a favor against him, that he would summon him to Jerusalem—while they lay in ambush along the road to kill him" (Acts 25:2-3). To his credit, Festus refused to give in to the Jew's plea for a change of venue. If they wanted to confront Paul, they would have to travel to Caesarea. Luke knew that the Jews wanted to kill Paul; did Festus also know of their sinister plot?

The court case before Festus involved at least three things. First, formal charges had to be given by the prosecutor. Second, the accusers would have to bring formal charges. Third, the case was then heard by the one with authority, in this case Festus, the procurator. Later in the chapter (verses 15-16) it is clear that Paul's detractors did, face to face, confront him.

The charges against Paul emerge from Acts 25:8: "Neither against the law of the Jews, nor against the temple, nor against Caesar have I offended in anything at all." Paul's preaching the gospel of Christ was perceived as an offense against Caesar and the Roman Empire. Largely, the Romans were reluctant to indict strictly on matters pertaining to religion; so, the political element was introduced. Festus was on safe legal ground when he offered Paul the opportunity to go to Jerusalem and make his defense there before the governor. Festus was under no obligation (other than his own lack of integrity) to use the Sanhedrin, but he could have done so. Festus, as was true of Felix, though, continued to court the favor of the Jews. Appearing in Jerusalem was the very thing Paul wanted to avoid. After all, he was safe because he had left Jerusalem; to return was dangerous. He makes a decision that would have far-reaching consequences for him, the church in Rome, and Christians everywhere. The consequences have continued for the last 2,000 years.

"So Paul said, 'I stand at Caesar's judgment seat, where I ought to be judged. To the Jews I have done no wrong, as you very well know. For if I am an offender, or have committed anything deserving of death, I do not object to dying; but if there is nothing in these things of which these men accuse me, no one can deliver me to them. I appeal to Caesar,'" (Acts 25:10-11). Paul knew that Festus knew that no wrong had been done against the Jews. The right of Roman citizenship was now exercised. Paul's appeal immediately stopped the current legal proceedings. The prisoner and his accusers would have to go to Rome. It was no little matter for someone to be sent to Rome. Clearly from what Luke tells us, much time lapsed before Paul even got there. The Roman government was under pressure to safely deliver prisoners to Caesar. We wonder what Festus now thought about Paul. Roman governors always wanted to avoid even the hint of trouble in their jurisdiction. Caesar is mentioned nine times in Acts 25. Yet, Paul's ultimate concern remained Jesus, King of Kings and Lord of Lords, the ultimate judge of all.

CHAPTER 80

The Hope of Israel

> "They knew me from the first, if they were willing to testify, that according to the strictest sect of our religion I lived a Pharisee. And now I stand and am judged for the hope of the promise made by God to our fathers."
> (Acts 26:5-6)

Rather disingenuously, Festus told Agrippa that he lacked specific charges to make against Paul. The Jews had been specific. What Festus really lacked was evidence to back up the charges against Paul. Will it be different with Agrippa?

One wonders how Paul could be "happy" to stand before Agrippa. King Agrippa was one of many in a long line of the Herods. Herod the Great had sought to kill the baby Jesus. His son, Antipas (the "fox") beheaded John the Baptist. Agrippa I, grandson of Antipas, killed James the son of Zebedee. At least two things were true when Paul began his defense; one, Agrippa was thoroughly acquainted with the Jews and their religion; two, the Herods had consistently stood against what was true and right. Before such a one, Paul now appears.

Paul gives a short history of his life. His early life was spent in Jerusalem, sitting at the feet of Gamaliel (Acts 22:3); evidently, this was common knowledge. Paul would have known what the Law said, prescribed, forbade, etc. So, he has now done something wrong regarding the temple? Paul had lived as a Pharisee; his zealousness was undisputed. Now, he is on trial for the very thing he has been working for, namely, the hope of Israel. Paul shared with all other Jews the hope and anticipation of the Messiah—something the Old Testament clearly spoke about. Even though misguided, the twelve tribes of Israel expected the Messiah. "To this promise our twelve tribes, earnestly serving God night and day, hope to attain. For this hope's sake, King Agrippa, I am accused by the Jews" (Acts 26:7). Luke mentions (Acts 23:6 and 24:21) the resurrection and the Sadducees; this sect of the Jews was the real culprit in bringing charges against Paul. Now, to Agrippa, Paul says: "Why should it be thought incredible by you that God raises the dead?" (Acts 26:8). What reason could the king and others give that would mitigate against the resurrection of Christ?

Moving next to his violent persecution of Christians, Paul's past was well known. Now, though, Paul was no longer on the same side as Agrippa; the persecutor was now the preacher. His Damascus road experience, among other things, resulted in Paul's commission to be the Apostle to the Gentiles. What the Lord told Paul to do, he did. Paul began immediately to preach the gospel that at one time he hated. Harking back to his Jewish roots, Paul said his life and work and preaching were clearly in line with what Moses and the prophets had said; Agrippa could not claim ignorance of such information.

"Then Agrippa said to Paul, 'You almost persuade me to become a Christian'" (Acts 26:28). "This remark shows that Agrippa saw very clearly the aim of the apostle" (McGarvey, *Acts*, 258). Some say that Agrippa was being sarcastic, or that he spoke ironically, or that he was angry. Whatever we say about his reaction to Paul, it is clear that Paul was doing what the Lord told him to do, namely, preach the gospel! The charges against Paul were false; had he not appealed to Caesar, Paul could have gone free. Instead he now packs his bags for a trip to Rome.

CHAPTER 81

I Believe God

"And when it was decided that we should sail to Italy, they delivered Paul and some other prisoners to one named Julius, a centurion of the Augustan Regiment."
(Acts 27:1)

Acts 27 is a fascinating chapter. Luke's narrative captures the imagination of his readers, as Paul and other prisoners began their journey toward Rome. The sea-tossed ship, the extreme weather conditions, and the constant threat of shipwreck all cause us to ask: What will happen to Paul? Would he finally realize his long-held desire to visit Rome, the epicenter of the world, the city of kings, chariot races, theaters, and temples? Will he stand before Caesar? Would he finally meet fellow believers, perhaps some of whom who had been in Jerusalem on Pentecost? Or, would he perish along the way?

It must have been a comfort to Paul to have his friends, Luke and Aristarchus, with him. Aristarchus had traveled with Paul to Jerusalem (Acts 20:4); and he is identified by Paul as a fellow-prisoner (Colossians 4:10). Luke's presence is sprinkled throughout the book of Acts (note the use of "us" or "we"). Luke had been with Paul for the preceding two years; was he gathering material for his two-volume history of Christ and His church? And was Aristarchus a prisoner along with Paul, in a symbolical sense? Whatever the case was, still, it was good for Paul to have these two men share the trials of this tempestuous journey.

Acts 27:14 says, "But not long after, a tempestuous head wind arose, called Euroclydon." Contrary winds were a part of Paul's voyage. McGarvey comments on this verse, saying, "The name Euraquilo, given to this wind, is equivalent to North-easter, and it indicates the direction from which it blew. It rushed down suddenly from the mountain top in Crete, and struck the vessel" (*Acts*, 266). Many sermons have been preached using "Contrary Winds" as their title. Yes, the contrary winds of life beat and blow upon us. Certainly this was true for Paul. Bad weather continued; cargo was thrown overboard; lives were in jeopardy.

How fortunate for all that this noted prisoner was on board. Paul assures his fellow travelers that they would not perish; his confidence came from the Lord. "Therefore take heart, men, for I believe God that it will be just as it was told me" (Acts 27:25). Don't be afraid. Keep up your courage. Such words, many times over, were real to Paul. How often did he recount the Lord's initial charge: "Therefore take heart, men, for I believe God that it will be just as it was told me. But the Lord said to him, 'Go, for he is a chosen vessel of Mine to bear My name before Gentiles, kings, and the children of Israel. For I will show him how many things he must suffer for My name's sake?'" Those words again were real.

Paul had faith in God. But he also, while trusting the power of God, was sensible. It was time to eat. "And when he had said these things, he took bread and gave thanks to God in the presence of them all; and when he had broken it he began to eat" (Acts 27:35). In the midst of the storm Paul took time to thank God for this needed food. Trusting in God, doing what is right, not being foolish—all of Paul's actions demonstrate that he was someone who truly believed in God. Two-hundred seventy-six people heard Paul pray. And they ate together with gladness.

CHAPTER 82

Now When We Come to Rome

"Now when we came to Rome, the centurion delivered the prisoners to the captain of the guard; but Paul was permitted to dwell by himself with the soldier who guarded him."
(Acts 28:16)

Shipwreck, snakebite, healing the sick—Paul's journey to Rome was exciting to say the least. Imagine, too, the wonder of those traveling with Paul. How had they all survived the ordeal of traversing the chilly waters of the Mediterranean? Surely, something extraordinary was going on. No longer was Paul a murderer; now he was a "god."

Arriving first at Puteoli, the Gulf of Naples, Paul enjoyed the company of brethren before moving on to Rome. Then others came to meet the Apostle, coming south of Rome to the Appii Forum and the Three Inns (a personal note: it is quite fascinating to walk in close proximity to the same roads Paul and others walked on 2000 years ago). The greeting party encouraged Paul. He was soon speaking with the leaders of the Jews.

Paul had done nothing against his own people the Jews. He had not violated any Jewish customs. The Romans could not find any guilt in him. It was because of the Jews that Paul finally had to make his appeal to Caesar. Still, Paul did not hold this outcome against his fellow Jewish brethren. He said again that it was "for the hope of Israel I am bound with this chain" (Acts 28:20). The leaders had not received any formal charges against Paul; in fact, they were curious about Paul's work and associations in the kingdom of Christ.

Acts 28:23 says, "So when they had appointed him a day, many came to him at his lodging, to whom he explained and solemnly testified of the kingdom of God, persuading them concerning Jesus from both the Law of Moses and the Prophets, from morning till evening." Paul was speaking to the *Jew first*. This audience was familiar with the Law of Moses and the Prophets; their reaction was mixed. Yet, when Paul quotes Isaiah 6:9-10, a passage that speaks about God including Gentiles in the kingdom, the crowd thinned considerably. Acceptance or rejection of the message did not deter Paul from continuing his work.

"Then Paul dwelt two whole years in his own rented house, and received all who came to him, preaching the kingdom of God and teaching the things which concern the Lord Jesus Christ with all confidence, no one forbidding him" (Acts 28:30-31). From reading Acts alone, we wonder what exactly happened to Paul. For two years he had the freedom to receive visitors and to preach the gospel. Was he beheaded at the end of the two years? Was he released, then traveled, then rearrested and then put to death? Luke is silent about these matters. Paul told Timothy, "At my first defense no one stood with me, but all forsook me. May it not be charged against them" (2 Timothy 4:16). Does this tell us that Paul stood trial but his accusers could not make their case? Did he leave Rome and travel to more places to preach?

On the Damascus Road the Lord told Paul to preach to the Gentiles. He did that with a consuming passion, continuing until the time for his departure came. "Therefore let it be known to you that the salvation of God has been sent to the Gentiles, and they will hear it!" (Acts 28:28). He said that the Gentiles would listen. And he was willing to preach to them, even if it meant going to Rome.

www.ingramcontent.com/pod-product-compliance
Lightning Source LLC
LaVergne TN
LVHW020930090426
835512LV00020B/3294